Joan:

To one of the most beautiful and caring daughters of light there could be. Thank you so for always be such an inspiration and example to me. I am so excited to work with you next year!

Love you much,

Jill McDonald

DAUGHTERS OF LIGHT

*Compiled
by*
Carol Lynn Pearson

BOOKCRAFT INC.
SALT LAKE CITY, UTAH

5th Printing, 1976

LITHOGRAPHED IN U.S.A.

PUBLISHERS PRESS
SALT LAKE CITY, UTAH

AUTHOR'S PREFACE

In a day when women are reaching for new powers, the Latter-day Saint woman can rejoice in hers. For she has been given, by virtue of her membership in the Church and her companionship with the Holy Ghost, powers beyond the wildest dreams of the most aspiring women of our day.

This book is *one* study, in *one* direction, intended to give the Latter-day Saint woman an affirmation of some of the things God has given her. She need not be deceived by those who would tell her she is not in a position of strength, for her powers are enormous. For the needs of her own life, for the development of her own relationship with the Lord, and for her righteous influence in the lives of her husband, her children, and all people within her possibility of touching — for all of these things she has full opportunity to receive any gift of the Spirit available to the children of God.

The early sisters of the restored Church enjoyed these gifts in abundance. It is my hope that in reading of the spiritual heights attained by them, we too might be moved, as Paul wrote to Timothy, to "stir up the gift of God which is in thee," and consequently to realize our full spiritual citizenship in the gospel of Jesus Christ.

There are two things this book is not intended to do. The first is to suggest deviation from or rebellion against the authorized chain of priesthood authority. All men and women are subject to the administrative order that exists within the Church and within the home. Our goal should be to use this order in a proper manner, to the end that *all*, men and women alike, will grow to their fullest spiritual capacity.

The second thing this book is not intended to do is to encourage seeking after a sign. There is much wisdom in the Lord's message to Thomas that "blessed are they that have not seen, and yet have believed." Our concern should be that we cultivate the spiritual quality of our own lives to the extent that we are enjoying consistently the gifts of knowledge, wisdom, faith, testimony, and that we might be in a position, should the need arise and should it be the will of the Lord, to exercise whatever other spiritual gift he might give us, even to the working of miracles.

The need for strong men is great. And the need for strong women is also great. Not proud — but neither weak. Let us join hands, brothers and sisters together, lending our mutual spiritual strengths to the building of the Kingdom of God. To that end this book is dedicated.

Carol Lynn Pearson

The time is coming when no man or woman will be able to endure on borrowed light. Each will have to be guided by the light within himself. If you do not have it, you will not stand.

Heber C. Kimball

CONTENTS

THE FAMILY OF LIGHT

Kindled into the family
That sparked the sun,
We came —
With suns and moons and stars
In us forever.

And the Mother
Who nurtures new light
In the warmest of all wombs,
And the Father
Who holds in his hands
The growing glow and blows it brighter —
Together placed us in another room.

It is dark here.
Deep within element,
We dim and dim.
And to slim the ray
That might find its way out,
We hand-craft clever bushels
Of modest, fashionable fears.

But long darkness is untenable
To one whose patriarchal line shines gold,
And we yearn for the burning
To begin again.

We have had too much night.
Shall we —
Shall we together shed our bushels
And stand revealed —
Sons and daughters of light?

With the impartial love
Of perfect parents
Wishing to lighten and lift,
To each of us, son or daughter,
Has been given a gift —

Chapter One

THE GIFTS IN GENERAL AND WOMEN IN PARTICULAR

In one of his final statements in the *Book of Mormon,* the Prophet
Moroni says, "And now I speak unto all the ends of the earth — that
if the day cometh that the power and gifts of God shall be done away
among you, it shall be because of unbelief."[1]

Unbelief did darken the land, but with the restoration of the gospel
came a renewal of the gifts of the Spirit. James E. Talmage gives an
excellent summary:

> The Latter-day Saints claim to possess within the Church all the sign-
> gifts promised as the heritage of the believer. They point to the unim-
> peached testimonies of thousands who have been blessed with direct
> and personal manifestations of heavenly power; to the once blind, deaf,
> dumb, halt, and weak in body, who have been freed from their infir-
> mities through their faith and by the ministrations of the Holy
> Priesthood; to a multitude who have voiced their testimony in tongues
> with which they were naturally unfamiliar, or who have demonstrated
> their possession of the gift by a phenomenal mastery of foreign lan-
> guages when such was necessary to the discharge of their duties as
> preachers of the word of God; to many who have enjoyed personal
> communion with heavenly beings; to others who have prophesied in
> words that have found speedy vindication in literal fulfillment; and
> to the Church itself, whose growth has been guided by the voice of
> God, made known through the gift of revelation.[2]

The great justice of the heavenly plan is evidenced in the fact that
these gifts have been and are available without reservation to all worthy
children of God, men and women alike. Every soul who believes, is
baptized by authority and receives the Holy Ghost, is eligible to receive
the gifts of the Spirit.[3]

Ordination to the priesthood, while bringing with it wonderful opportunities for spiritual development and blessings, is not a pre-requisite to enjoyment of the gifts of the Spirit. In the "Lectures on Faith" we read:

> The principle of power which existed in the bosom of God, by which the worlds were framed, was faith; and that it is by reason of this principle of power existing in the Deity, that all created things exist; so that all things in heaven, on earth, or under the earth, exist by reason of faith as it existed in Him.[4]

This power of faith is available to both men and women, depending on their obedience to the laws upon which faith is predicated.

The Prophet Joseph Smith made some remarkable statements to the sisters at the time he organized the Relief Society in Nauvoo. He said to them, as recorded by Eliza R. Snow in the minutes, that "the keys of the kingdom are about to be given to them that they may be able to detect anything false, as well as to the Elders."[5] He went on to describe the spiritual powers available to them, saying, "If you live in accord with your privileges, angels cannot be restrained from being your associates."[6]

It is, in fact, not only the privilege, but the solumn duty of every Latter-day Saint woman, married or unmarried, to cultivate the spiritual powers that lie within her own soul. A statement of Heber C. Kimball should be given occasional review by every member of the Church:

> The time is coming when no man or woman will be able to endure on borrowed light. Each will have to be guided by the light within himself. If you do not have it you will not stand.[7]

Many Latter-day Saint women have lived by the light within themselves, powerfully and righteously. President Joseph F. Smith once said of Eliza R. Snow:

> Others who were associated with her were, many of them, as moonlight and starlight compared to the sunlight of her dynamic presence and her sublime powers. She walked not in the borrowed light of others but faced the morning unafraid and invincible.[8]

Other of our great priesthood leaders have encouraged the spiritual attainments of the sisters and have admitted their deep admiration of them. Matthew Cowley once wrote:

> All the saving power in this Church is not in the priesthood. It is just as much or more in those who don't hold the priesthood, meaning, of course, the women, than there is in us who bear it.[9]

Here, then, are the women — some of them — sister Saints who cultivated their own light, and lived by it.

To speak
The perfect word,
Mind and mouth momentarily free
From the stilted syllables
Of mortality —

Chapter Two

THE GIFT OF TONGUES
AND
THE GIFT OF INTERPRETATION OF TONGUES

Seen in proper perspective, the gifts of speaking in tongues and interpreting tongues, while indeed dramatic, are actually among the lesser of the gifts. In their place, however, they were and they continue to be valuable tools in the building of the Kingdom.

In the early days of the restored Church, these gifts were manifest widely and enjoyed by both men and women. The Prophet Joseph, in telling of a meeting held January 22, 1833, relates that he and "all the Elders spake in tongues, and several members, both male and female, exercised the same gift."[1]

It was not uncommon for the gift of tongues to be manifest in the meetings of the sisters of the Relief Society. In the minutes of that organization for April 18, 1842, we read:

> Counselor Cleveland stated that she many times felt in her heart what she could not express in her own language and as the Prophet had given us liberty to improve the gifts of the Gospel in our meetings, and feeling the power resting upon her, she desired to speak in the gift of tongues, which she did in a powerful manner.

> Mrs. Sessions arose and gave the interpretation of what counselor Cleveland had spoken in an unknown tongue and said that God was well pleased with this society.[2]

The early Saints evidently abused this gift somewhat, for Joseph was moved on several occasions to restrain them. "Be not so curious about tongues," he said. "The gifts of God are all useful in their places, but when they are applied to that which God does not intend, they prove an injury, a snare, and a curse instead of a blessing."[3]

The following instances show the righteous use of the gifts of speaking in and interpreting tongues, as manifest in the lives of the early sisters.

Zina — Speaker And Interpreter

A sister whose gift of tongues was widely recognized was Zina D. Huntington Young, who became the third President of the Relief Society. While still a young girl, she was baptized by Hyrum Smith and confirmed under the hands of Hyrum Smith and David Whitmer.

Soon after this, the gift of tongues rested upon me with overwhelming force. I was somewhat alarmed at this strange manifestation, and so checked its utterance. What was my alarm, however, to discover that upon this action upon my part, the gift left me entirely, and I felt that I had offended that Holy Spirit by whose influence I had been so richly blessed.

I suffered a great deal in my feelings over this matter, and one day while mother and I were spinning together, I took courage and told her of the gift I had once possessed, and how, by checking it I had lost it entirely.

Mother appreciated my feelings, and told me to make it a matter of earnest prayer, that the gift might once more be given to me.

I walked down to a little spring in one of the meadows, and as I walked along I mused on my blessing and how I had turned away the Spirit of God. When I reached the spring, I knelt down and offered up a prayer to God and told Him if He could forgive my transgression, and give me back the lost gift, I would promise never to check it again, no matter where or when I felt its promptings.

I have kept this vow, but it has been a heavy cross at times, for I know that this gift is the least of all gifts, and it is oftentimes misunderstood and even treated lightly by those who should know better. Yet it is a gift of God, and should not be despised by him who receives it, but magnified to its extent, even as the lowest grade of the priesthood is the least of all, and yet it needs be magnified as earnestly as are the higher and greater offices.

From the day I received the sweet testimony of the Spirit, when grasping the precious Book of Mormon in my hands to my breast, I have never doubted nor faltered in my faith. I know this is the Church and Kingdom of God, and I rejoice in putting my testimony before the daughters of Zion, that their faith may be strengthened, and that the good work may roll on.[4]

*Throughout her long life, Zina kept her vow and used the gifts
as the Spirit moved her. The* Woman's Exponent *describes some of
these occasions.*

The absence of the pioneers on their journey to the Rocky Mountains
was a time of great anxiety to those who remained behind, and especially
to those whose fathers, husbands and brothers were members of that
memorable company. The sisters held regular meetings, to pray and
exercise faith for the pioneers. At these meetings Sister Zina was a
regular attendant, and she is largely endowed with spirituality, which
qualifies her admirably as an active worker in such a capacity. She
has, perhaps, as perfect a gift of interpretation of tongues as any person
in the Church, for although her opportunities for education in language
have been limited, and she is not a poet or rhymer, yet she gives the
interpretation of hymns, psalms and sacred songs in the most musical
and happy manner, without thought or hesitation. There is something
divinely beautiful in thus rendering, by the gift of inspiration, words
uttered in an unknown tongue.[5]

"Sister Lydia, Rise Up"

*Lydia Bailey, who became the wife of Newel Knight, received
with rejoicing the ordinance of baptism when the gospel was
presented to her. It was Joseph Smith who baptized her, and who
was instrumental in her receiving the gift of tongues.*

The evening of this day (which was the seventh day the Prophet
had been there and came on Monday, October 24, 1833), the family
were all seated around the wide, old-fashioned fire-place in the parlor
listening to the Prophet's words and full of rejoicing.

"I would be so glad if some one who has been baptized could receive
the gift of tongues as the ancient Saints did and speak to us," said
Moses Nickerson.

"If one of you will rise up and open your mouth it shall be filled,
and you shall speak in tongues," replied the Prophet.

Every one then turned as by a common instinct to Lydia, and said
with one voice, "Sister Lydia, rise up."

And then the great glory of God was manifested to this weak but
trusting girl. She was enveloped as with a flame, and unable longer
to retain her seat, she arose and her mouth was filled with the praises
of God and His glory. The spirit of tongues was upon her, and she
was clothed in a shining light, so bright that all present saw it with
great distinctness above the light of the fire and the candles. [6]

A Black Sister Receives The Gift Of Tongues

*Jane Elizabeth James, a black convert to the Church, made
her way to Nauvoo, met Joseph Smith, and impressed him with
her courage in surmounting obstacles. Sister James reports that
Joseph brought Emma to her and said, "Sister Emma, here is
a girl that says she has no home, haven't you a home for her?"
Emma replied, "Why, yes, if she wants one." Sister James lived
in the Prophet's home until his death. She traveled to
Salt Lake City and was a well-known member of the Church
there. She and her brother enjoyed reserved seats near the front
and center of the Tabernacle for Sunday services. President
Joseph F. Smith spoke at her funeral. Her story is preserved in a
"Life Sketch," written in 1893.*

When a child only six years old, I left my home and went to live with a family of white people. Their names were Mr. and Mrs. Joseph Fitch, they were aged people and quite wealthy. I was raised by their daughter. When about fourteen years old I joined the Presbyterian Church, yet I did not feel satisfied. It seemed to me there was something more that I was looking for. I had belonged to the church about eighteen months when an Elder of the Church of Jesus Christ of Latter-day Saints was traveling through our country and preached there. The pastor of the Presbyterian Church forbid me going to hear them as he had heard I had expressed a desire to hear them; but nevertheless I went on a Sunday and was fully convinced that it was the true gospel he presented and I must embrace it.

The following Sunday I was baptized and confirmed a member of the Church of Jesus Christ of Latter-day Saints. About three weeks after while kneeling at prayer the gift of tongues came upon me, and frightened the whole family who were in the next room. [7]

Mother Whitney Sings In The Adamic Tongue

*Ann Whitney was widely known among the early Saints
for her gift of singing in tongues. In his journal Wilford Woodruff
writes of a visit to his home of Sister Whitney and Eliza R. Snow.*

We passed a pleasant evening together, and before they left they sang in tongues in the pure language which Adam and Eve spoke in the Garden of Eden. This gift was obtained in the Kirtland Temple through a promise of the Prophet Joseph Smith. He told Sister Whitney if she would rise upon her feet she should have the pure language. She did so, and immediately began to sing in tongues. It was nearer to heavenly music than anything I ever heard. [8]

In her biographical sketch, Assistant Church Historian
Andrew Jensen tells more of Sister Whitney's gift.

She was among the first members of the Church to receive the gift of tongues, which she always exercised in singing. The Prophet said that the language was the pure Adamic tongue, the same that was used in the Garden of Eden, and he promised that if she kept the faith, the gift would never leave her. It never did, and many who heard her sing never forgot the sweet and holy influence that accompanied her exercise of this heavenly gift. The last time she sang in tongues was on the day she was 81 years old. It was at the home of Sister Emmeline B. Wells, the latter having arranged a party, in honor of Mother Whitney's birthday. At a meeting held in the Kirtland Temple, Sister Whitney sang in tongues and Parley P. Pratt interpreted, the result being a beautiful hymn descriptive of the different dispensations from Adam to the present age. [9]

Sister Whitney occasionally edified the sisters of the Relief Society
with her gift. The Salt Lake Stake Relief Society Record reports
such an event on July 17th, 1880.

Sister Whitney then sang one of her sweet songs on Zion in the language which was spoken and sung (the Prophet Joseph said) by our first parents in the Garden of Eden. Sister Snow explained that Joseph Smith told Mother Whitney if she would use the gift with wisdom it should remain with her as long as she lived. Sister Zina then gave the interpretation, the theme of which was rejoicing and praise to the Great Author and Giver of Good. [10]

15

A Young Girl Bears Testimony In Several Languages

The gifts of the Spirit were being enjoyed by the Saints in all parts
of the vineyard. A sister identified only as a young girl working
for Ann Howell Burt had an unusual experience with the gift
of tongues in England.

This girl had been brought up among the poorest of the poor and had never had an opportunity of learning anything, but she was gifted with wonderful musical ability. She had joined the Church and was a good, true girl.

About a week after her confirmation into the Church, she went to meeting and the gift of speaking in tongues was given to her in a most wonderful degree. When she arose to her feet she began to sing a most beautiful song. The words and music were blended harmoniously, and although it was in an unknown tongue and no one present understood it, everybody was delighted, and the spirit that went with it was sweet and heavenly. The gift of interpretation was also given her, and she interpreted it herself in song. No one knew before then that the girl could sing; but after that she often delighted the people.

One day a gentleman named John McMamout, from India, came to visit Ann's father. He was highly educated and spoke many different languages. Brother Howell invited the stranger to dine with them, that he might have an opportunity of explaining the Gospel, which was his delight. The gentleman accepted the invitation, and an interesting Gospel conversation ensued. Afterwards, as was the daily custom, Brother Howell rang a bell for the members of his household to assemble for devotion in a certain room which had been set apart for that purpose. After Brother Howell had prayed and said amen, the girl arose and spoke in a tongue unknown to all present except the stranger, who understood and interpreted. She had told him that the "Mormon" Church was the Church of Christ and that there was no other. The girl spoke to him in several different languages, which he understood. He marveled greatly. [11]

An Uneducated Collier's Wife Speaks In Hebrew

Another English convert to the Church had a similar experience.
This story took place in 1854.

16

Many of the members of the White Chapel Branch of the Church enjoyed the gifts of the Spirit — the gift of tongues, the interpretation of tongues, visions, healings, and prophecy. Notably among these was the wife of a poor collier. This lady was uneducated and uncultured as to worldly learning; consequently her speech was ungrammatical and faulty, but when speaking under the inspiration of God, her language was lucid and elegant. One sabbath day the members of the White Chapel Branch were surprised to see a neatly dressed gentleman, a stranger, take a seat in the congregation. After the customary devotional exercises, the sacrament was administered and then the services were given over to testimony bearing.

Among those who arose to speak was the collier's wife referred to. As she began to speak the stranger listened with wrapt attention. Following this speaker, another member arose and gave the interpretation in English. When the services were concluded the gentleman approached the collier's wife and addressed her in an unknown tongue. In blank amazement the poor woman shook her head and informed the visitor that she could not understand what he said. It was now his turn to show amazement. "What!" said he, "You do not understand me. I am a Hebrew scholar, and an officer in the British Army stationed in India. I have just listened to you speak the most perfect Hebrew I ever heard spoken, and now when I ask you a simple question in that tongue, you pretend not to understand me." "Oh," she said, "I was speaking by the gift of tongues and do not understand what I said." The Hebrew scholar departed without further word, imagining he was being duped . . . .

The import of the message as given in tongues lay bare a plot then brewing among the native of India against the British Indian government, and was no doubt given for the express benefit of the officer. [12]

Eliza R. Snow — "In The Mud Rejoicing"

The Saints at Winter Quarters seem to have received a special outpouring of spiritual gifts to sustain them. Selected excerpts from the diary of Eliza R. Snow are moving testimony of this. A glimpse into the twelve days prior to her leaving for Utah shows the sisters receiving great comfort from the gift of tongues and from other of the gifts as well.

Tuesday, June 1. This is truly a glorious time with the mothers & daughters of Zion, altho' thrust out from the land of our forefathers & from endearments of civiliz'd life. This forenoon I made a cap for sis. Peirce; in the afternoon I visited at sis. Miller's, in com(pany) of Priscinda, Zina, sis. Chase, Cristene etc. After supper sis. Whitney, Kimball (and) Sessions came in and we had a spiritual feast in very deed. Spent the eve. at br. Leonard's with Priscinda, Zina & Sarah — great instruction was brought forth . . . .

17

Wednesday, June 2. Spent the after(noon) with Lucy in com(pany) of Zina, Loisa & Emily. E(mily) & myself spoke in the gift of tongues. In the eve. met at Harriet's; had a good time — Sis. Young join'd me in a song of Zion.

Thursday, June 3. Sis. Sess(ions), Kim(ball), Whit(ney), & myself spent the eve. at Sarah Ann's (Kimball's) — had a pow'rful time — deep things were brought forth which were not to be spoken.

Friday, June 4. We had a very pleasant visit at br. Leonard's. Present: br. Joseph Y(oung) & wife, br. Sess(ions) & wife, sis. Whitney, Kimball, etc. I blest sis. Young.

Saturday, June 5. Fath(er) Sess(ions) leaves for the wilderness. I attended meeting at sis. Leavitt's.

Sunday, June 6. Had a glorious time at sis. Young's. Present: sis. Whit(ney), Kim(ball), Chase, etc. I had forgotten to mention a time of blessing at sis. K(imball)'s the day after we met at Sarah's. Sis. Sess(ions) & myself blest Helen (Mar Whitney). I spoke & she interpreted. I then blest the girls in a song, singing to each in rotation.

In the eve. that we met at Harriet's, sis. Young told me she thought (it) wisdom for me to go to the west, inasmuch as I could go so comfortable with br. Peirce. Sis. P(eirce) had mention'd her wish for me to go with them, in his absence, but he had not yet decided whether his means would permit.

Monday, June 7. Met at sis. Woodruff's in the afternoon — at br. Leonard's in the eve. Moth(er) Butler receiv'd the gift of tongues. Sis. Scovil present.

Tuesday, June 8. Met at Lyman Whitney's, stay'd in the eve., had a heavy shower of rain — went home with Loisa & Z(ina) in the mud rejoicing.

Wednesday, June 9. Visited with Zina, Martha, L(oisa), E(mily), Lucy, Eliza & Sarah. After supper we had a glorious time. Sis. Peirce came in — sis. Thompson, M. Jones & Francis. Before we retir'd to rest, Margaret, Martha, Loisa, Susan & Lucy receiv'd the gift of tongues.

Thursday, June 10. In the mor(ning) met sis. Chase at Clarissa's — blest her little daughter which was born last Tu(esday). Told Harriet she would get the gift of interpretation in the eve. In the aft(ernoon) call'd at sis. Woodru(ffs) & Priscinda's & went to br. Moore's where sis. Whit(ney)'s girls met, sent for Zina, Harriet came with her. Sis. Richards, Rhoda, Emeline, Anna, & one of sis. M(arkham)'s daughters spoke in the gift for the first time. Took supper with S(arah) Ann K(imball). While there Lucy W. came in — she receiv'd the gift. We then went into sis. K(imball)'s — Helen, Sarah Ann, Genet, Harriet S., sis. K(imball) spoke for the first time in the gift of tongues — H. Cook interpreted.

Friday, June 11. Sent for Harriet — we commenc'd improving in the gifts — Helen got the interpretation, also sis. W. Mary Ellen spoke in a new tongue, sis. Pack also — we had a time not to be forgotten. In the aft. met at Clarissa's — sis. Snow receiv'd the gift before we left Loisa's. We had a glorious time — sis. Leavitt & M(argaret) Peirce spoke in the gift & I could truly say that my heart was fill'd to overflowing with gratitude to my Father in heaven.

Saturday, June 12. Bade farewell to many who seemed dearer to me than life &, seated in the carriage with sis. P(eirce), M(argaret) & E(li), I took my departure from Winter Quarters. [13]

After she was established in the valley, and indeed for the rest of her life, Eliza was a strong spiritual force among the Saints. This interesting excerpt comes from her diary of 1848.

Saturday, January 1. A dinner party at Br. Miller's. After dinner, Moth(er) M(iller) arose and express'd her wish for the sis(ters) to proceed in their order of blessing, having call'd them in by the consent of her husband, requested Sis. Sess(ions) to pray. Sis. Sess(ions) arose & said she was subject to Sis. M(iller) while under her roof & was willing to act in accordance, &c. She pray'd, after which I arose & bless'd Sis.

M(iller) & was follow'd by Sis. Holmes, Howd, Sessions, three of Sis. M(iller)'s daughters [two of whom rec(eived) the gift of tongues], Love & Abbott — five breth(ren) present, 4 of whom spoke, Br. Jackman remarking that there was more intelligence in the hearts of the sis(ters) that aft. than in the hearts of all the crown'd heads of Europe. By request of his wife, Br. M(iller) dismiss'd the meet(ing) — sent for Clara & spent the eve with Fath(er) Sess(ions). [14]

Jane Grover Confounds Indians In Their Own Tongue

An occasion in which the gift of tongues was of great practical value occurred near Council Bluffs as the Saints were on their way westward. It is told in the journal of Jane Grover, later Mrs. Stewart, and happened when she was a girl of seventeen.

One morning we thought we would go and gather gooseberries. Father Tanner (as we familiarly called the good, partriarchal Elder Nathan [John] Tanner), harnessed a span of horses to a light wagon, and, with two sisters by the name of Lyman, his little granddaughter, and me, started out. When we reached the woods we told the old gentleman to go to a house in sight and rest himself while we picked the berries.

19

It was not long before the little girl and I strayed some distance from the rest, when suddenly we heard shouts. The little girl thought it was her grandfather, and was about to answer, but I restrained her, thinking it might be Indians. We walked forward until within sight of Father Tanner, when we saw he was running his team around. We thought nothing strange at first, but as we approached we saw Indians gathering around the wagon, whooping and yelling as others came and joined them. We got into the wagon to start when four of the Indians took hold of the wagon-wheels to stop the wagon, and two others held the horses by the bits, and another came to take me out of the wagon.

I then began to be afraid as well as vexed, and asked Father Tanner to let me get out of the wagon and run for assistance. He said, "No, poor child; it is too late!" I told him they should not take me alive. His face was as white as a sheet. The Indians had commenced to strip him — had taken his watch and handkerchief — and while stripping him, were trying to pull me out of the wagon. I began silently to appeal to my Heavenly Father.

While praying and struggling, the spirit of the Almighty fell upon me and I arose with great power; and no tongue can tell my feelings. I was happy as I could be. A few moments before I saw worse than death staring me in the face, and now my hand was raised by the power of God, and I talked to those Indians in their own language. They let go the horses and wagon, and all stood in front of me while I talked to them by the power of God. They bowed their heads and answered "Yes," in a way that made me know what they meant. The little girl and Father Tanner looked on in speechless amazement. I realized our situation; their calculation was to kill Father Tanner, burn the wagon, and take us women prisoners. This was plainly shown me. When I stopped talking they shook hands with all three of us and returned all they had taken from Father Tanner, who gave them back the handkerchief, and I gave them berries and crackers. By this time the other two women came up, and we hastened home.

The Lord gave me a portion of the interpretation of what I had said, which was as follows:

"I suppose you Indian warriors think you are going to kill us? Don't you know the Great Spirit is watching you and knows everything in your heart? We have come out here to gather some of our father's fruit. We have not come to injure you; and if you harm us, or injure one hair of our heads, the Great Spirit shall smite you to the earth, and you shall not have power to breathe another breath. We have been driven from our homes, and so have you; we have come out here to do you good, and not to injure you. We are the Lord's people and so are you; but you must cease your murders and wickedness; the Lord is displeased with it and will not prosper you if you continue in it. You think you own all this land, this timber, this water, all the horses: Why, you do not own one thing on earth, not even the air you breathe — it all belongs to the Great Spirit." [15]

20

Singing In The Red Man's Tongue

*Another story of a woman being blessed with the gift of
tongues in the face of danger from Indians is told by Irene King
Read. The central character in this event is her grandmother,
Matilda Robison King, who was living with her husband at Cove Fort.*

My grandfather, Thomas Rice King, lived for a time at this Cove Fort. It was during a period of much trouble with the Indians. In 1867 the fort had been built to accommodate ten or twelve families. It was built of stone, with big, thick walls and heavy gates. My grandparents, with other families, lived in this fort for some time, while the Indians were on the war-path.

One day the men left the women and children to go into the canyon for a load of wood. As the Indians had not been bothering for some time, and the men didn't expect to be gone very long, they left the gate unbolted. Soon after they left several war-painted and vicious looking Indians stalked through the gate and into the Fort. The poor, frightened women caught up their children and hurried to my grandmother's room. The Indians followed them to the door, banged loudly on it and demanded food. The terror stricken women did not dare refuse, and so allowed them to enter while they quickly set food on the table. Grandmother was able to conceal her fright more than the other women. As the warriors started gulping down their food, one of them, who appeared to be their leader, or chief, motioned to her and grunted, "You sing now." Grandmother hesitated, not knowing what to do. She felt she could never control her voice for the fright she felt, hidden though it was. But at the second more gruff command, the sisters, fearing for their own and their children's lives, pleaded with her. "Oh, please, Sister King, sing for them." As the Indians began again to grunt, "Hurry up. Sing!" she started to sing the first song that came to her mind, hardly realizing that it was a Latter-day Saint hymn, "O Stop and Tell me, Red Man." After the first verse she paused, but the Indians, who had stopped eating to listen, demanded more. The women were looking at her in astonishment.

When she had sung the entire four verses of the hymn, the Indians, to the amazement and relief of the little group, got up from the table and filed silently out of the door and out of the gate. The women flew to my grandmother. "Why, Sister King, we didn't know you knew the Indian language." Grandmother stared at them. "Know the Indian language? Why, I don't." "But you sang that entire song in their language," they said excitedly. "That's why they got up and left. They understood every word you sang to them!"

And so she had God's spirit directing her. The message of that hymn went straight to their black, superstitious hearts, and they left the frightened white people to go back to their camps and ponder the words of the song sung by my Grandmother King. It used to be in our hymn books, but so many of the old hymns have been dropped that I will give the words here.

O STOP AND TELL ME, RED MAN

O stop and tell me, Red Man, who are you, why you roam.
And how you get your living; have you no God, no home?
With stature straight and portly, and decked in native pride,
With feathers, paint and brooches, he willingly replied:

"I once was pleasant Ephraim, when Jacob for me prayed,
But O, how blessings vanish, when man from God has strayed!
Before your nation knew us, some thousand years ago,
Our fathers fell in darkness, and wandered to and fro.

And long they've lived by hunting, instead of works and arts,
And so our race has dwindled to idle Indian hearts.
Yet hope within us lingers, as if the spirit spoke:
'He'll come for your redemption, and break the Gentile's yoke.'

'And all your captive brothers from every clime shall come
And quit their savage customs, to live with God at home.
Then joy will fill your bosoms and blessings crown your days,
To live in pure religion and sing our Maker's praise.'" [16]

"Plant And You Shall Reap"

*The pioneers that arrived in Utah during the first few years
of settlement were in the front ranks of the battle to make the
desert blossom. They needed all the comfort and courage
they could muster. Many stories are told of the Saints receiving
divine encouragement, such as this one by Mrs. R. C. Atwood.*

I will here relate an incident of our seed time: My husband had taken a lot of land near what is now called the Sugar House Ward. He took his team and went to plow and prepare it for the seed. In due time he went to plant his corn and he found the ground as dry as ashes to a great depth. It seemed impossible to him for the seed ever to germinate in such a soil. He planted the seeds, however, knowing that if he did not plant he surely could not reap. He came home at night hungry, faint and weary. I was also very weary from the labors of the day. We had planted a garden near the house and I brought water from the City Creek in pails every day to water it (the creek then flowed down the east side of Main Street); and the water made the ground as hard as an adobe. We partook of our scanty meal and prepared to retire to rest. We then bowed ourselves before the Lord to implore His blessing to rest upon us.

His Spirit did rest upon us powerfully in the gift of tongues and the interpretation of the same. My husband commenced praying in his own language and suddenly he broke out in an unknown tongue. I understood what he said. At first it was a reproof from the Lord for our unbelief. It was thus: "Have I not brought you all this way from the land of your enemies to this goodly land? and I will bless this land for my people's sake, if they will put their trust in me, and it shall bring forth in great abundance of grass, grain and vegetables of every kind, fruit also, of the choicest kind, and your tables shall be loaded with the best fruits of the earth. Only put your trust in me. Plant and you shall reap."

We arose and retired to rest, but not to sleep. Sleep had departed from our eyes. We were filled with wonder, love and admiration. We could not doubt more. We went to work with fresh courage. The earth yielded more and more each succeeding year, and in the year 1850, my husband reaped forty bushels of wheat per acre. Our garden also produced choice vegetables. [17]

22

Spiritual Power Of Anna Widtsoe

*Anna Karine Gaarden Widtsoe, born in Norway, traveled to
Utah as a widow with two sons. Her accomplishments, spiritual
and temporal, are recorded by her devoted son, John A. Widtsoe.*

She grew rapidly in spiritual power. Under Gospel influence her
comprehension was quickened, and a prophetic view of the future was
developed. She walked in close communion with the spiritual forces
which she invited by eager, never-failing attention to her duties as she
learned to understand them. One day in her ward testimony meeting
she arose, her face glowing with a new light, and spoke in an unknown
tongue. Another faithful sister arose and interpreted Sister Widtsoe's
remarks. Both had received that day the gift of tongues. The widow
had the same gift on several later occasions. She grew more and more
as an inspired women of Israel. [18]

A Reproof Sent In Tongues

*The gift of tongues was often sent as a means of bringing some
helpful message. Such appears to be the case in an incident in the
life of Anna Maria Isaacson Whiting, related by her daughter,
Martha Whiting Brown Berry.*

Mother was told in her Patriarchal Blessing that she would be blessed
with the "Gift of Tongues." One Sunday when we had fast meeting
from two o'clock to four o'clock in the afternoon, I was sitting by Mother
in church. The house was full and as the Bishop opened services he
said in all the years he had been Bishop he had never felt so humbled
by the Spirit of God. We all felt it and soon a sister rose to bear her
testimony and suddenly she told the congregation that she would like
to speak in tongues, which she did. A little later another woman prayed
for an interpretation. Soon I saw my Mother start to weep. She gave
me the babe she was holding, rose to her feet and told us she had
received the interpretation. She said we had been told by the sister
that if the people in Mapleton would stop finding fault and backbiting
one another the typhoid fever would be taken from their midst. After
that it was discovered to be in the water and was brought under control. [19]

Interpretation Of A Blessing To Hyrum G. Grant

*On the first Sunday of January, 1900, Apostle John W. Taylor
and his wife Nellie had in their home a gathering of patriarchs
and other Church officers. After dinner they were expressing to
one another their feelings about the gospel and their desire to do as
the Lord wanted them to do. A nephew of "Aunt Nellie" tells of a
blessing given that night and of its fulfillment.*

John Kennison, Patriarch, got up and walked across the room and
put his hands on the head of Hyrum G. Grant and gave him a blessing,
speaking in tongues; and when the blessing was concluded, he resumed
his seat. And there was a moment or two of silence in the room, and
then John W. Taylor nudged Aunt Nellie with his elbow and said, "Nellie,
you have the interpretation." She whispered back and said, "Yes, I
know, John, but I'm just frightened to death." And he said, "You stand
on your feet, and as soon as you start to speak that fear will leave
you." So she stood up and she said . . . "Brother Grant has received
a very remarkable blessing. The Lord has told him that He had a work
for him to do — that he's called to do — and that if he would live
true and faithful to the gospel, that the Lord would preserve him and
he would be able to fulfill this calling that was for him." She said that
the evil one would seek to destroy him, and that his protection would
come about by living the principles of the Gospel . . . .

Some years later, after they had established a colony in Canada,
John W. Taylor had taken Aunt Nellie up there. . . . I was living in
West Bountiful in the same ward where Hyrum G. Grant lived at that
time. He had a very serious sickness — in those days it was called
yellow jaundice. His body turned almost completely black. And I
remember going down there and saw that they had scattered straw
for about a quarter of a mile on the dirt road in front of his house
so that the wagons would make less noise going back and forth. He
was very dangerously ill. Finally the sickness reached a point where
they thought that it would be impossible for him to recover. So the
family sent wires out to such members as were absent.

One of his brothers, Frank Grant, was up in Canada. He received
the wire and had to ride a considerable distance to take the train. He
thought, well, I'll ride around by Aunt Nellie's and see if she has any
word to send down to the folks in Utah. So he went by her place
and when he spoke to her, she said, "Yes, Frank, I do have something.
I want you to go to your mother as soon as you arrive and tell her
that her son is not going to die, but to remember the blessing that
was given to him on this occasion as mentioned."

So he went to the old home; and when he arrived, all the family
were there (including Heber J. Grant, who later became president),
the wives, and the doctor. Frank stepped up behind his mother and
put his arms around her and said, "Mother, I have a message for you

from Aunt Nellie. She said to tell you that your son is not going to die, but to remember the blessing that he was given on the occasion mentioned." About this time, the doctor who had been kneeling at the head of the bed, arose as he thought Hyrum G. Grant had expired. He got up to turn to the mother and wives that were there, but as he looked back on Hyrum G. Grant, he noticed just a little flicker of his eyelid; so he knew from that, that the spirit had not left his body . . . . It was President Grant, who said let's administer to him, which they did; and from that very low spark of life (the doctor had actually thought the spirit had left), he returned — he regained his health and strength.

And as a boy, I lived there and knew him as the stake president. So he fulfilled that mission that was given to him by Patriarch Kennison in tongues and interpreted by Nellie E. Taylor. [20]

To see,
Cutting through calendars and clocks,
Possessing power
To invite tomorrow to share
The present hour —

Chapter Three

THE GIFT OF PROPHECY

The scriptures verify that prophecy is a gift that women may rightfully possess. The Book of Acts speaks of "four daughter, virgins, which did prophesy." [1] James E. Talmage affirmed this as well, saying, "The ministrations of Miriam and Deborah show that this gift may be possessed by women also." [2]

In the latter days many women have enjoyed this gift. Certainly the first prophetess of this dispensation was Lucy Mack Smith, mother of the Prophet Joseph. Wilford Woodruff wrote of Lucy as a "noble mother and prophetess." [3] And the sisters in Utah who published the *Woman's Exponent* wrote that one who knew Lucy Smith "can scarcely think of her except as a prophetess." [4]

Many other lesser-known women also received, according to their own needs, the gift of prophecy.

"He Will Have Power Over All His Enemies"

*In 1838, after Joseph and other leaders were taken prisoner
by an army and taken to Independence, Lucy Smith was in
despair. She recounts the special help sent to her in this
circumstance.*

For some time our house was filled with mourning, lamentation, and woe; but, in the midst of my grief, I found consolation that surpassed all earthly comfort. I was filled with the spirit of God, and received the following by the gift of prophecy: "Let your heart be comforted concerning your children, they shall not be harmed by their enemies; and in less than four years, Joseph shall speak before the judges and great men of the land, for his voice shall be heard in their councils. And in five years from this time he will have power over all his enemies."

This relieved my mind, and I was prepared to comfort my children. I told them what had been revealed to me, which greatly consoled them. [5]

The Saints Delivered By Prophecy And Faith

In the spring of 1831 Lucy Smith was chosen to lead a company of eighty Saints from Waterloo to Kirtland. The trip down the Erie Canal by flatboat had taken five days and was a nightmare of hunger and exposure. At Buffalo the harbor was ice-locked and the Saints were stranded. They began complaining loudly and arguing with one another. William Smith approached Lucy and said, "Mother, do see the confusion yonder; won't you go and put a stop to it!"

I stepped into their midst. "Brethren and sisters," said I, "We call ourselves Saints, and profess to have come out from the world for the purpose of serving God at the expense of all earthly things; and will you, at the very onset, subject the cause of Christ to ridicule by your own unwise and improper conduct? You profess to put your trust in God; then how can you feel to murmur and complain as you do! You are even more unreasonable than the children of Israel were; for here are my sisters pining for their rocking-chairs, and brethren from whom I expected firmness and energy, declare that they positively believe they shall starve to death before they get to the end of the journey. And why is it so? Have any of you lacked? Have not I set food before you every day, and made you, who had not provided for yourselves, as welcome as my own children? Where is your confidence in God? Can you not realize that all things were made by him, and that he rules over the works of his own hands? And suppose that all the Saints here should lift their hearts in prayer to God, that the way might be opened before us, how easy it would be for him to cause the ice to break away, so that in a moment we could be on our journey! . . . Now, brethren and sisters, if you will all of you raise your desires to heaven, that the ice may be broken up, and we be set at liberty, as sure as the Lord lives it will be done."

At that instant a noise was heard, like bursting thunder. The captain cried, "Every man to his post." The ice parted, leaving barely a passage for the boat, and so narrow, that, as the boat passed through, the buckets of the water-wheel were torn off with a crash, which, joined to the word of command from the captain, the hoarse answering of the sailors, the noise of the ice, and the cries and confusion of the spectators, presented a scene truly terrible. We had barely passed through the avenue, when the ice closed together again, and the Colesville brethren were left in Buffalo, unable to follow us.

As we were leaving the harbor, one of the bystanders exclaimed, "There goes the Mormon company! That boat is sunk in the water nine inches deeper than ever it was before, and, mark it, she will sink — there is nothing surer." In fact, they were so sure of it that they went straight to the office and had it published that we were sunk, so that when we arrived at Fairport, we read in the papers the news of our own death. [6]

Lydia Knight Dreams Of A Visit From Joseph

Prophetic dreams were not uncommon in the early Church.
Joseph Smith records such a one in his history.

After our departure from Colesville, after the trial, the Church there were very anxious, as might be expected, concerning our again visiting them, during which time Sister Knight, wife of Newel Knight, had a dream, which enabled her to say that we would visit them that day, which really came to pass, for a few hours afterwards we arrived; and thus was our faith much strengthened concerning dreams and visions in the last days, foretold by the ancient Prophet Joel. [7]

Dream Of A Visit From The Elders

Sarah Pea Rich, wife of Charles C. Rich, tells of a prophetic
dream that preceded her baptism into the Church.

In the summer of 1835 two Mormon elders came to preach in our home, by request of my father. He had met them in the town of Bellville, nine miles away. At that time I, together with my parents, was a member of the Reformed Methodist Church.

The two elders came and held a meeting and preached on the first principles of the gospel, and related to the people about there being a prophet in their church, and told us about the *Book of Mormon* and the angel appearing to the Prophet. All this was new to the people. It was in the afternoon that they held their meeting; so my father asked them to stay all night — which invitation they accepted. They were on their way to Kirtland, Ohio, some five hundred miles from where we then lived.

After supper was over a number of neighbors gathered, to hear these strange men talk. Feeling anxious to see the *Book of Mormon* they had told us about, I asked one of the leaders if I could see the book, and I asked the company to excuse me for the evening. I retired to my room and spent the rest of that evening and most of the night reading it. I was truly astonished at its contents. The book left an impression on my mind never to be forgotten. It appeared to be open before my eyes for weeks afterwards.

The next morning the men left for Ohio. Our family had many things to say about this strange people, but the things the men told us left a deep impression on our minds, not easy to be forgotten. We did not think we should ever meet with the men again. But after they had been gone six weeks, I had a dream concerning them. I dreamed on Friday night that they would come to our house the next evening, just as the sun was going down, and that they would first come in sight at the end of a long lane in front of the house. I also dreamed that I met them on the porch and of a remark made by them and one made by myself in answer — which I will relate later on.

In the morning father and mother went to Bellville. At breakfast I had asked father if he would not try to be home early. He answered, "Why are you so particular? Is your young man coming?" I said, "No, father, but those two Mormon elders will be here to-night." "Why," asked father, "have you heard from them?" I said, "No, but I dreamed last night that they would be here, and I feel sure it will be so." Father said I must be crazy, for those men were hundreds of miles away. But I insisted: "Father, hurry home this evening, for I am sure they will come." He only laughed, and he and mother went off to town. Then I said to my sister, "Let's prepare, for those men will surely be here." She, too, laughed at me. But as it was Saturday, we went to work baking and preparing for Sunday, as was our custom.

As the day passed, I began to look, once in a while, down the lane for those men. Sure enough, just as the sun was setting, they made their appearance, just where I dreamed I first saw them. I met them on the porch, and bade them the time of day. "I have been looking for you to come," I said. "Why," one of them answered, "had you heard we were coming?" "No," I said, "I dreamed last night that you would come, and I felt sure you would be here." "Well," said one of the elders, "we had a dream that we were to return here and baptize you and build up a church in this region." I answered, "Well, that is something in the future." I bade them take chairs and be comfortable, for my parents would soon be home.

In a very short time my father and mother drove into the yard. As I was standing on the porch, my father said to me, "Well, Sarah, where are your Mormon elders?" I told him they were in the house, at the same time they stepped out on the porch, to meet him. Father was struck with astonishment, as he remembered what I had told him in the morning about my dream. [8]

Prophecy Of The Healing And Mission Of
Daniel Tyler

Daniel Tyler, a lame elder, received great encouragement
from a prophecy given to him in tongues. A year later he left to
fill a mission in Switzerland.

I was at the time going on crutches, with a broken leg, and having but little hope of ever being able to walk. The leg was badly fractured, and by getting out of place and having to be reset caused the bones to be very slow in knitting together. It was about seven months before I could bear any weight upon my broken limb. While in this condition, I went on my crutches to a little prayer meeting in a private house, there being no public meeting house then built in the ward.

In going to the meeting, my worst fears of always being a cripple had loomed up before me like a great mountain, and, like Jonah, I felt that "it was better for me to die than to live." This was a weakness in me, of course, but so it was.

After the meeting was opened, Sister More arose and began to speak in tongues. She addressed her remarks to me, and I understood her as well as though she had spoken the English language. She said: "Your leg will be healed, and you will go on a foreign mission and preach the gospel in foreign lands. No harm shall befall you, and you shall return in safety, having great joy in your labors."

31

This was the substance of the prophecy. It was so different from my own belief and the fears of many others that I was tempted not to give the interpretation, lest it should fail to come to pass. The Spirit, however, impressed me and I arose, leaning upon my crutches, and gave the interpretation.

Not long afterwards I was told in a dream what to do to strengthen my fractured limb, and it began to receive strength immediately, and in the short space of about one week I dispensed with my crutches and walked with a cane. [9]

Widow Smith's Journey To The West

One of the few well-known stories of prophecy and faith
evidenced by the early Mormon sisters is this one of Mary
Fielding Smith, widow of Hyrum, as she dramatically triumphed
over all odds on her journey to the West.

At the death of the patriarch the care of the family fell upon his widow, Mary Smith. Besides the children there were several helpless and infirm people, whom for various charitable reasons the patriarch had maintained; and these also she cared for, and brought through to the valley the major part of them, under unusually trying circumstances.

Passing over the incidents of her journey to Winter Quarters, after the expulsion from Nauvoo, we came at once to her heroic effort from Winter Quarters westward. In the spring of 1848 a tremendous effort was made by the Saints to emigrate to the valley on a grand scale. No one was more anxious than Widow Smith; but to accomplish it seemed an impossibility, for although a portion of her household had emigrated in 1847, she still had a large and, comparatively, helpless family — her sons John and Joseph, mere boys, being her only support. Without teams sufficient to draw the number of wagons necessary to haul provisions and outfit for the family, and without means to purchase, or friends who were in circumstances to assist, she determined to make the attempt, and trust in the Lord for the issue. Accordingly every nerve was strained, and every available object was brought into requisition. Cows and calves were yoked up, two wagons lashed together, and a team barely sufficient to draw one was hitched on to them, and in this manner they rolled out from Winter Quarters some time in May. After a series of the most amusing and trying circumstances, such as sticking in the mud, doubling teams up all the little hills, and crashing at ungovernable speed down the opposite sides, breaking wagon-tongues and reaches, upsetting, and vainly trying to control wild steers, heifers, and unbroken cows, they finally succeeded in reaching

the Elk Horn, where the companies were being organized for the plains.

Here Widow Smith reported herself to President Kimball as having "started for the valley." Meantime, she had left no stone unturned or problem untried, which promised assistance in effecting the necessary preparations for the journey. She had done to her utmost, and still the way looked dark and impossible.

President Kimball consigned her to Captain ———'s fifty. The captain was present. Said he:

"Widow Smith, how many wagons have you?"

"Seven."

How many yokes of oxen have you?"

"Four," and so many cows and calves.

"Well," said the captain, "it is folly for you to start in this manner; you never can make the journey, and if you try it you will be a burden upon the company the whole way. My advice to you is, to go back to Winter Quarters and wait till you can get help."

Widow Smith calmly replied: "Father ———"(he was an aged man), "I will beat you to the valley, and will ask no help from you, either!"

This seemed to nettle the old gentleman, and it doubtless influenced his conduct toward her during the journey.

While lying at Elk Horn she sent back and succeeded in buying on credit, and hiring for the journey, several yoke of oxen from brethren who were not able to emigrate that year, and when the companies were ready to start she and her family were somewhat better prepared for the journey, and rolled out with lighter hearts and better prospects than favored their egress from Winter Quarters.

As they journeyed on the captain lost no opportunity to vent his spleen on the widow and her family; but she prayerfully maintained her integrity of purpose, and pushed vigorously on, despite several discouraging circumstances.

One day, as they were moving slowly through the hot sand and dust, in the neighborhood of the Sweetwater, the sun pouring down with excessive heat, towards noon, one of Widow Smith's best oxen lay down in the yoke, rolled over on his side, and stiffened out his legs spasmodically, evidently in the throes of death. The unanimous opinion was that he was poisoned. All the hindmost teams of course stopped, the people coming forward to know what was the matter. In a short time the captain, who was in advance of the company, perceiving that something was wrong, came to the spot. Probably no one supposed for a moment that the ox would recover, and the captain's first words on seeing him were:

"He is dead, there is no use working with him; we'll have to fix up some way to take the widow along; I told her she would be a burden upon the company."

Meantime Widow Smith had been searching for a bottle of consecrated oil in one of the wagons, and now came forward with it, and asked her brother, Joseph Fielding, and the other brethren, to administer to the ox, thinking that the Lord would raise him up. They did so, pouring a portion of oil on the top of his head, between and the back of the horns, and all laid hands upon him, and one prayed, administering the ordinance as they would have done to a human being that was sick. In a moment he gathered up his legs, and at the first word arose to his feet, and traveled right off as well as ever. He was not even unyoked from his mate.

On the 22d of September the company crossed over "Big Mountain," when they had the first glimpse of Salt Lake Valley. Every heart rejoiced, and with lingering fondness they gazed upon the goal of their wearisome journey. The descent of the western side of "Big Mountain" was precipitous and abrupt, and they were obliged to rough-lock the hind wheels of the wagons, and, as they were not needed, the forward cattle were turned loose to be driven to camp, the "wheelers" only being retained on the wagons. Desirous of shortening the next day's journey as much as possible, they drove on till a late hour in the night, and finally camped near the eastern foot of the "Little Mountain." During this night's drive several of Widow Smith's cows, that had been turned loose from the teams, were lost in the brush. Early next morning her son John returned to hunt for them, their service in the teams being necessary to proceed.

At an earlier hour than usual the captain gave orders for the company to start, knowing well the circumstances of the widow, and that she would be obliged to remain till John returned with the lost cattle. Accordingly the company rolled out, leaving her and her family alone. Hours passed by ere John returned with the lost cattle, and the company could be seen toiling along far up the mountain. And to human ken it seemed probable that the widow's prediction would ingloriously fail. But as the company was nearing the summit of the mountain a cloud burst over their heads, sending down the rain in torrents, and throwing them into utter confusion. The cattle refused to pull, and to save the wagons from crashing down the mountainside, they were obliged to unhitch, and block the wheels. While the teamsters sought shelter, the storm drove the cattle in every direction, so that when it subsided it was a day's work to find them and get them together. Meantime, as noted, John had returned with the stray cattle, and they were hitched up, and the widow and family rolled up the mountain, passing the company and continuing on to the valley, where she arrived fully twenty hours in advance of the captain. And thus was her prophecy fulfilled. [10]

Prophetic Blessings Of Eliza R. Snow

34

At her funeral, Eliza R. Snow's many gifts were detailed, one of them being the gift of prophecy. Throughout her life she used this gift in blessing the Saints. Sarah M. Kimball records the first of such blessings given by Eliza.

The first person that ever Sister E. R. Snow laid her hands upon to bless was Lydia Granger, mother of S.M. Kimball. In the home of S.M.K., Nauvoo, Ill. It came about in this way. We were conversing about the Bible and about children arising and blessing their parents. The writer said, "Sister Snow, you come and lay your hands on my head and bless me." She arose and looking at my mother said, "It seems more proper to bless the elder first." I said, "Do so." There were only three of us present, but the occasion was memorable. I note it here because it comes to my mind in connection with the anniversary of her 80th birthday. Many thousands have received blessings under her hands and have rejoiced in the promises she has made them. [11]

Carrie Smith was among the many who received such a blessing from Eliza. Her husband was called to preside as bishop over the little settlement of Paradise, near Logan.

Three years later she was asked by Sister Eliza R. Snow to preside over the Young Ladies' Mutual Improvement Association then organized in that ward for the first time, and as if to strengthen and fortify her for other trials yet to come, she blessed her by using the gift of tongues, greatly to the surprise of Sister Smith who had never heard the gift before, and the blessings there given have been verified. [12]

Prophecy Concerning The Apostleship Of
Heber J. Grant

*President Heber J. Grant bears witness to the prophetic
powers of Eliza R. Snow in regard to a significant event in
his own life.*

When I was a child, in a Relief Society meeting, Eliza R. Snow,
by the gift of tongues, and Zina D. Young, by the interpretation thereof,
promised that child playing on the floor — in the home where Grandma
Whitney, my mother, Eliza R. Snow, Zina D. Young, Clara Kimball
and other leading Relief Society sisters in early days were meeting —
that that child should grow to manhood and become an apostle of the
Lord Jesus Christ. My mother often said to me: "Heber, behave yourself,
and you will some day be one of the apostles in the Church." I always
laughed at her and said: "Get it out of your head. Every mother thinks
her son will be the president of the United States or something wonderful. I have no ambitions in that regard."

When I was called to be one of the apostles she asked me if I remembered that meeting in the home of the late William C. Staines on the
corner of South Temple and Fifth East. I told her I did. "Do you remember
anything that was said?" I replied, "No." "Well," she said, "Do you
remember Aunt Eliza talking to you on the floor?" I said, "Yes, but
I did not understand it."

"Of course, you did not, because she spoke by the gift of tongues."
Then she said: "Do you remember anything that Aunt Zina said?" "Yes,
I do, mother. I remember that she lifted her hand and said that I would
become a great big man."

So when I became tall I used to think of it occasionally, that Aunt
Zina said I would be a big man. My mother responded: "She said nothing
of the kind; she said you would be a great big man in the Church
of Jesus Christ of Latter-day Saints, that you would be an apostle."
That is why I have told you, knowing that the gift of tongues was
in the Church. [13]

35

A Wife's Blessing To Her Husband

*President Grant relates another story concerning a prophecy
given by a woman and its subsequent fulfillment – a very
touching story of a wife exercising her own spiritual powers in
behalf of her husband.*

Many years ago I was a ruined man financially. Struggling to meet
the interest on my debts of more than a hundred thousand dollars,

I worked assiduously, often far into the night. For four long years I owed between twenty-five and thirty thousand dollars upon which I could not pay one cent of interest.

On one occasion, during my financial difficulties, I came home at one o'clock in the morning. My wife was sitting up waiting my return. When I came in she greeted me with these words: "Heber, you do not use tea, coffee, tobacco or liquor, but you are breaking the Word of Wisdom because of your working the way you do, even to a greater extent than if you used tea and coffee; and I am not sure that you are not breaking it more than if you used tobacco. It is a shame the way you are over-working and over-taxing your strength."

She stopped speaking, and then, she was given the gift of tongues and, in a strange language, she gave me a blessing, the spirit of which I felt and knew, although I could not understand a word of what she said. I wept for joy.

When she ceased speaking she asked, "Do you have the interpretation?"

I answered, "No." And then we knelt down and prayed that we might be given the meaning of this heavenly message. It came to us in these words, in substance: That I should live to cancel every obligation I owed and to possess a comfortable home, and be free from debt; and that I should live to proclaim the gospel in many lands and climes."

At that time I owned not a home and had never been upon a foreign mission. This was over thirty-seven years ago.

It was not long after this that my wife died, as I have mentioned. And now I come to the fulfilment of the promises made to me through her in tongues.

In 1897 I underwent an operation for appendicitis in an advanced stage. Nine physicians were present and eight of them said I could not live. The ninth, as he himself later told me, "Took a chance on my recovery" because of the exceptionally strong heart he found I possessed. Blood poison set in and I was in the last stage of its development. I told my doctor to let me know if I had one chance in fifty to recover and that if greater odds than these were against me, to advise me to send for my secretary. He advised me to have her come and take my last story for, he said, I hadn't a chance to live.

In the meantime my present wife came in the room and told me that a very short time before, my deceased wife, who gave me the blessing in tongues years ago, had appeared to her and told her that she need not worry; that I was not going to die then and that my mission on earth was not yet ended.

When she related this circumstance to me I recalled the promise made to me in tongues, that I should live to lift my voice in many lands and climes, proclaiming the restoration of the gospel. And I knew then that that promise would be fulfilled. Then I turned to her and said, "Isn't it wonderful that you and I know more than the doctor, and that, although, blood poisoning has developed to the third stage, I do not have to die and shall live to fulfill the promise made by the gift of tongues by my wife, who has told you that my mission is not yet ended."

I give to the Lord Almighty the credit and the glory for the preservation of my life, for it is by his power that I am here today. The promises made to me in tongues by my companion before her death, and the promise she made to my present wife, by a heavenly visitation, have literally been fulfilled.

In 1927 I was able to pay off the last dollar of my indebtedness, with five hundred dollars in the bank to my credit. I had been able to acquire a comfortable home and it was free from debt. And, since my operation, through the grace and the power of God, I have proclaimed the restoration of the gospel in many lands and climes. I have lifted up my voice in the Hawaiian Islands, in far-off Japan, in England, Ireland, Scotland, Wales, Germany, Holland, France, Belgium, Italy, Switzerland, Norway, Sweden, Denmark, Canada, Mexico; from Portland, Maine, to Portland, Oregon; from the Canadian line to Florida, bearing witness that I know, as I know that I live, that God lives; that Jesus is the Christ; that Joseph Smith was a prophet of the true and living God; that the Gospel, commonly called "Mormonism" is in very deed, the gospel of Jesus Christ; with every gift, grace, power and blessing that were enjoyed in former days. [14]

Zina D. H. Young Blesses Her Grand-daughter

A grand-daughter of Zina D. H. Young, Mary Jacobs Wilson,
tells of receiving a prophetic blessing from her grandmother and
of its fulfillment.

In 1896, Grandmother made the trip from Salt Lake to West Weber, Weber County, Utah, the day before New Years to spend the rest of the holidays with her son Chariton and family. Visiting her children and their families was one of her greatest joys in life. After dinner was finished and the dishes put away, we all gathered in the parlor. My father asked his precious mother what she would like done at that time. My mother's brother, George Rigby, had just returned from a mission to England and was with us that evening. Grandmother stated that she would be very pleased to hear him tell of his missionary experiences while away. Then the conversation drifted to a discussion of the principles of the Gospel. Soon each one present felt a choice spirit in their midst, and Grandmother arose as the gift of tongues had come to her, and gave my father, Henry Chariton, a most beautiful blessing. This was followed by each one present receiving a blessing in the same manner. I was a baby less than a year old.

The bells and whistles at the depot in Ogden were heard seven miles away in West Weber by all present, ushering in the New Year. Often Mother told me that no one present thought they had been together more than an hour and they had enjoyed the rich, spiritual blessings of our Heavenly Father for five hours.

Mother often told me of this event, and when the interpretation was given, she learned that Grandmother had promised me that I would be a leader among women. In 1946 I was called to be a member of the Relief Society General Board and remained for eight years before moving to New York. For eighteen years I worked on the American Mothers Board and for one year was a member of the National Council of Women. This was evidence of a fulfillment of a prophecy given by Grandmother. [15]

Prophetic Sense Of Sisters In New Zealand

Matthew Cowley writes admiringly of the spiritual powers of the Saints in New Zealand. Many of the stories he tells concern the native sisters.

38

Now I remember when President Rufus K. Hardy of the First Council of the Seventy passed away. I was walking along the street of one of the cities in New Zealand, and one of our native members came up — a lady.

She said to me, "President Hardy is dead."

I said, "Is that so? Have you received a wire?"

She said, "No. I received a message, but I haven't received any wire." She repeated, "He's dead. I know."

Well, I always believed them when they told me those things. When I got back to headquarters, I wasn't there long when here came a cablegram which said that President Hardy had passed away the night before. But she knew that without any cablegram. She told me about it.

I got out of my car once in the city. I got out to do some window-shopping to get a little rest from driving. I walked around, and finally I went around a corner, and there stood a native woman and her daughter. The mother said to the daughter, "What did I tell you?"

I said, "What's going on here?"

The daughter said, "Mother said if we'd stand here for fifteen minutes you'd come around the corner." Now she didn't have any radio set with her, just one in her heart where she received the impression. [16]

To step
Beyond borders
Of the second estate
For a walk with angels —
To be,
Escorted for the instant,
Into immortality —

Chapter Four

THE GIFT OF REVELATION

It has generally been taught and understood in the Church that all members, men and women alike, may receive personal revelation according to their needs. Instruction for the Church at large will never come through an unauthorized person, but each member is entitled to divine guidance in relationship to his or her stewardship.

This was made clear in the early days of the Church, as recorded in the "Nauvoo Conference Minutes" of January, 1845: "Every member has the right of receiving revelations for themselves, both male and female."[1] The early Saints accepted this right with great faith, and enjoyed rich communication with the heavens through visions, dreams, voices, and other divine manifestations.

A Scene In The Heavens

Even without the laying on of hands for the Gift of the Holy Ghost, many people have beheld divine manifestations. Vilate Kimball, wife of Heber C. Kimball, tells of such an event in New York.

On the night of the 22nd of September, 1827, while living in the town of Mendon, after we retired to bed, John P. Green, who was then a traveling Reformed Methodist preacher, living within one hundred steps of our house, came and called my husband to come out and see the sight in the heavens. Heber awoke me, and Sister Fanny Young (sister of Brigham), who was living with us, and we all went out-of-doors.

It was one of the most beautiful starlight nights, so clear we could see to pick up a pin. We looked to the eastern horizon, and beheld a white smoke arise towards the heavens. As it ascended, it formed into a belt, and made a noise like the rushing wind, and continued southwest, forming a regular bow, dipping in the western horizon.

After the bow had formed, it began to widen out, growing transparent, of a bluish cast. It grew wide enough to contain twelve men abreast. In this bow an army moved, commencing from the east and marching to the west. They continued moving until they reached the western horizon. They moved in platoons, and walked so close the rear ranks trod in the steps of their file leaders, until the whole bow was literally crowded with soldiers.

We could distinctly see the muskets, bayonets, and knapsacks of the men, who wore caps and feathers like those used by the American soldiers in the last war with Great Britain. We also saw their officers with their swords and equipage, and heard the clashing and jingling of their instruments of war, and could discern the form and features of the men. The most profound order existed throughout the entire army. When the foremost man stepped, every man stepped at the same time. We could hear their steps. When the front rank reached the western horizon, a battle ensued, as we could hear the report of the arms, and the rush.

None can judge of our feelings as we beheld this army of spirits as plainly as ever armies of men were seen in the flesh. Every hair of our heads seemed alive.

We gazed upon this scenery for hours, until it began to disappear.

After we became acquainted with Mormonism, we learned that this took place the same evening that Joseph Smith received the records of the Book of Mormon from the Angel Moroni, who had held those records in his possession.

Father Young, and John P. Green's wife (Brigham's sister Rhoda), were also witnesses of this marvelous scene.

Frightened at what we saw, I said, Father Young, what does all this mean? He answered, Why it is one of the signs of the coming of the Son of Man.

The next night a similar scene was beheld in the west, by the neighbors, representing armies of men engaged in battle. [2]

An Angel Shows The Golden Plates To
Mother Whitmer

During the difficult period when Joseph Smith and Oliver
Cowdery were translating the Book of Mormon *in the Whitmer*
home, Mother Whitmer was granted the special privilege
of seeing the plates. The story is told by her son, David Whitmer.

My mother was going to milk the cows, when she was met out near the yard by the same old man (judging by her description of him), who said to her: "You have been very faithful and diligent in your labors, but you are tired because of the increase in your toil; it is proper, therefore, that you should receive a witness that your faith may be strengthened." Thereupon he showed her the plates. My father and mother had a large family of their own, the addition to it, therefore, of Joseph, his wife Emma and Oliver very greatly increased the toil and anxiety of my mother. And although she had never complained she had sometimes felt that her labor was too much, or at least she was perhaps beginning to feel so. This circumstance, however, completely removed all such feelings and nerved her up for her increased responsibilities. [3]

Angels Prepare Her For Zion

An English convert to the Church, identified only as "Nellie
Colebrook's mother, whose maiden name was Purce,"
experienced a very helpful manifestation in her girlhood.
She had a broken foot that was neglected and resulted in a twisted
knee. For eight years she was on crutches.

She turned to scripture reading. One idea haunted her continually — that of the "wedding garment," indeed she really worried and fretted about it and refused to accept the highly spiritualized sectarian version, insisting that it *was a veritable garment.*

After a severe illness of the nature of brain fever, from which she showed some signs of recovery, she had what we would call a vision. Twelve personages entered her room and passed around her bed, following one after another until her bed was surrounded. They each pointed to her as they walked, and the last one, who seemed to be the superior, stretched out his hand and laid it on her head. He told her among other things that they wore the wedding garment; that she should live and should go to "Zion." Told her what to use for her lame limb and how to use it. And while she gazed at them through the beautiful light that filled the room, they were gone. She was commanded not to tell all that was said to her, but that portion she did tell was considered a dream and accepted as a sure premonition of death.

The doctor very much desired to remove the crooked limb as she rallied from her illness, but she clung to her promises and insisted on using what the person in the vision prescribed, and in three months she was able to walk.

Being a very practical person, she did not spiritualize the promise that she should go to Zion, and was ready for the gospel when it came. If any proof or testimony was wanting to convince her that the Zion she had found on earth was that Zion named to her by the heavenly messenger, she had it when in the endowment robes, she beheld the wedding garment worn by the twelve angels. [4]

Angels On The Kirtland Temple

Prescindia Huntington enjoyed, along with her sister Zina,
a number of spiritual gifts. The Kirtland period especially
saw a rich outpouring of the Spirit upon many Saints.

In Kirtland, we enjoyed many very great blessings, and often saw the power of God manifested. On one occasion I saw angels clothed in white walking upon the temple. It was during one of our monthly fast meetings, when the saints were in the temple worshipping. A little girl came to my door and in wonder called me out, exclaiming, "The meeting is on the top of the meeting house!" I went to the door, and there I saw on the temple angels clothed in white covering the roof from end to end. They seemed to be walking to and fro; they appeared and disappeared. The third time they appeared and disappeared before I realized that they were not mortal men. Each time in a moment they vanished, and their reappearance was the same. This was in broad daylight, in the afternoon. A number of the children in Kirtland saw the same.

When the brethren and sisters came home in the evening, they told of the power of God manifested in the temple that day, and of the prophesying and speaking in tongues. It was also said, in the interpretation of tongues, "That the angels were resting down upon the house."

At another fast meeting I was in the temple with my sister Zina. The whole of the congregation were on their knees, praying vocally, for such was the custom at the close of these meetings when Father Smith presided; yet there was no confusion; the voices of the congregation mingled softly together. While the congregation was thus praying, we both heard, from one corner of the room above our heads, a choir of angels singing most beautifully. They were invisible to us, but myriads of angelic voices seemed to be united in singing some song of Zion, and their sweet harmony filled the temple of God.

We were also in the temple at the pentacost. In the morning Father Smith prayed for a pentecost, in opening the meeting. That day the power of God rested mightily upon the saints. There was poured out upon us abundantly the spirit of revelation, prophesy and tongues. The Holy Ghost filled the house; and along in the afternoon a noise was heard. It was the sound of a mighty rushing wind. But at first the congregation was startled, not knowing what it was. To many it seemed as though the roof was all in flames. Father Smith exclaimed, "Is the house on fire!"

"Do you not remember your prayer this morning, Father Smith?" inquired a brother.

Then the patriarch, clasping his hands, exclaimed, "The spirit of God, like a mighty rushing wind!"

At another time a cousin of ours came to visit us at Kirtland. She wanted to go to one of the saints' fast meetings, to hear some one sing or speak in tongues, but she said she expected to have a hearty laugh.

Accordingly we went with our cousin to the meeting, during which a Brother McCarter rose and sang a song of Zion in tongues; I arose and sang simultaneously with him the same tune and words, beginning and ending each verse in perfect unison, without varying a word. It was just as though we had sung it together a thousand times.

43

After we came out of meeting, our cousin observed, "Instead of laughing, I never felt so solemn in my life."[5]

Knowledge Of Joseph In Trouble

The devotion the early Saints felt for their leader, Brother Joseph, forged strong spiritual ties between them and him. An incident that illustrates this is found in the journal of Sarah S. Leavitt.

While I was at Juliette I was alone a praying. After continuing in prayer for some time I thought of Joseph and commenced praying for him. As soon as I spoke his name I burst into tears and my heart was filled with grief and I said, "Oh my God, what is the matter with Brother Joseph?" I learned afterward the mob had him, raving over him. I did not know at this time that there were any mobs gathered. We were at Juliette, Illinois, and the mob in Missouri, but the spirit manifested to me that he was in trouble. I prayed with all the power I had for the prophet of God. "The fervent and effectual prayer of a righteous man availeth much, saith the Lord."[6]

Testimony of Four Relief Society Presidents

The sisters who became the first four presidents of the
Relief Society after the Church moved to Utah each report an
unusual spiritual experience related to their conversion.

Eliza R. Snow:

On the 5th of April, 1835, I was baptized by a "Mormon" Elder, and in the evening of that day, I realized the baptism of the Spirit as sensibly as I did that of the water in the stream. I had retired to bed, and as I was reflecting on the wonderful events transpiring around me, I felt an indescribable, tangible sensation, if I may so call it, commencing at my head and enveloping my person and passing off at my feet, producing inexpressible happiness. Immediately following, I saw a beautiful candle with an unusual long, bright blaze directly over my feet. I sought to know the interpretation, and received the following, "The lamp of intelligence shall be lighted over your path." I was satisfied. [7]

Zina D. Huntington Young:

It was in the year 1831, and I was then but ten years old. . . .the rumor reached us that there was a prophet in a distant country, who had found a new and golden Bible. The very word "prophet" caught my father's ear and arrested his attention. He was anxious at once to go to this so-called "prophet" and test the strength of his claim.

A neighbor by the name of Joseph Wakefield, cooper by trade, was a companion of my father, and together they had discussed the matter of true and false religions for many an hour. When this rumor about the prophet reached us father and Mr. Wakefield had an earnest consultation as to which should go and see the man. That one should go was an accepted decision. After some talk, Mr. Wakefield thought he would be the better one to go, as he was not at work in the winter season, and my father, who was a wealthy farmer, always had stock to attend to even in the winter.

Mr. Wakefield went at once to Seneca County, saw the boy prophet, received a convincing testimony of the truth, and returned with a heart full of zeal, bearing with him a copy of the new Bible, or as it is properly called, the Book of Mormon.

I was going to school that winter, and so did not hear all the talk that was carried on at home after the return of Mr. Wakefield, but I knew in substance what report he had brought with him. One day on my return from school I saw the Book of Mormon, that strange, new book, lying on the window sill of our sitting-room. I went up to the window, picked it up, and the sweet influence of the Holy Spirit accompanied it to such an extent that I pressed it to my bosom in a rapture of delight, murmuring as I did so, "This is the truth, truth, truth!" [8]

Bathsheba W. Smith:

When I heard the Gospel I knew it was true; when I first read the Book of Mormon, I knew it was inspired of God; when I first beheld Joseph Smith I knew I stood face to face with a prophet of the living God, and I had no doubt in my mind about his authority. [9]

Emmeline Blanche Wells:

As we neared our destination in sailing up the Mississippi [Nauvoo], the elders were full of enthusiasm at the thought of seeing the Prophet again. But not once in all the conversation did I hear a description of his personal appearance. There were no photographs in those days, and I had not formed any idea of him except of his wonderful power. I think in looking back upon that time, I must have been in a state of mingled emotions of astonishment and awe, not knowing what I should do or say on my arrival.

At last the boat reached the upper landing, and a crowd of people were coming toward the bank of the river. As we stepped ashore the crowd advanced, and I could see one person who towered away and above all the others around him; in fact I did not see distinctly any others. His majestic bearing, so entirely different from any one I had ever seen (and I had seen many superior men) was more than a surprise. It was as if I beheld a vision; I seemed to be lifted off my feet, to be as it were walking in the air, and paying no heed whatever to those around me. I made my way through the crowd, then I saw this man whom I had noticed, because of his lofty appearance, shaking hands with all the people, men, women and children. Before I was aware of it he came to me, and when he took my hand, I was simply electrified— thrilled through and through to the tips of my fingers, and every part of my body, as if some magic elixir had given me new life and vitality. I am sure that for a few minutes I was not conscious of motion. I think I stood still, I did not want to speak, or be spoken to. I was overwhelmed with indefinable emotion.

Sister Gates came to me and said, "I'll introduce you to the Prophet Joseph now, he is here."

I replied, "I don't want to be introduced to him."

She was astonished, and said curtly, "Why you told me how desirous you were of meeting him."

I answered, "Yes, but I've seen him and he spoke to me."

"But he didn't know who you were!"

I replied, "I know that but it does not matter," and Sister Gates walked away without another word of explanation. I was in reality too full for utterance. I think had I been formally presented to the

Prophet, I should have fallen down at his feet, I was in such a state of ecstacy. The one thought that filled my soul was, I have seen the Prophet of God, he has taken me by the hand, and this testimony has never left me in all the "perils by the way." It is as vivid today as ever it was. For many years, I felt it too sacred an experience even to mention. [10]

Visitation From A Loved Sister

Hannah Cornaby, a writer and poet in early Utah, tells of an event that happened in 1836 when she was a girl of fourteen. Her sister Lydia, "the joy of our hearts and home for eleven years," died.

I mourned so deeply that my health became impaired. Our family physician prescribing change of air and scene, my alarmed parents decided to act upon his advice; meanwhile I was praying to God for help to control my grief, desiring again to see my beloved sister; and this desire was granted me.

One Sunday afternoon, feeling too unwell to go to church, I remained at home, the other members of the family attending. Thus alone, my thought reverted to my sister; when lo! she stood before me, as when in perfect health and loveliness. My first impulse was to embrace her, but she moved from me, saying, "No, dear, you cannot." I was disappointed at this, and tried again to clasp her in my arms; but she again assured me I could not, and I had to be content to talk to her at a distance. I asked her if she lived in Heaven; she replied, "I am where Jesus is, will that satisfy you?" I said, "Yes," and asked how her clothes had been kept so well. She replied, "You remember, that while the children of Israel traveled in the wilderness, their clothes did not wax old; mine are preserved on the same principle." After some further conversation, she disappeared, keeping her face towards me until she vanished from sight. During her stay, and after she left, I was not in the least alarmed. I knew she had come from the spirit world to gratify my longing desire to see her. On their return, I told my parents what had happened and they thought it was a dream, but I knew I was awake at the time, although, at my mother's request, I afterwards told it as a dream. [11]

46

Amanda Smith At Haun's Mill

One of the most inspiring stories of personal revelation received in dire need is that of Sister Amanda Smith at the time of the Haun's Mill massacre in October, 1838. Surviving the slaughter, Sister Smith returned to the scene in search of her husband and three sons.

Passing on I came to a scene more terrible still to the mother and wife. Emerging from the blacksmith shop was my eldest son, bearing on his shoulders his little brother Alma.

"Oh! my Alma is dead!" I cried, in anguish.

"No, mother; I think Alma is not dead. But father and brother Sardius are killed!"

What an answer was this to appal me! My husband and son murdered; another little son seemingly mortally wounded; and perhaps before the dreadful night should pass the murderers would return and complete their work!

But I could not weep then. The fountain of tears was dry; the heart overburdened with its calamity, and all the mother's sense absorbed in its anxiety for the precious boy which God alone could save by his miraculous aid.

The entire hip joint of my wounded boy had been shot away. Flesh, hip bone, joint and all had been ploughed out from the muzzle of the gun which the ruffian placed to the child's hip through the logs of the shop and deliberately fired.

We laid little Alma on a bed in our tent and I examined the wound. It was a ghastly sight. I knew not what to do. It was night now . . . .

The women were sobbing, in the greatest anguish of spirit; the children were crying loudly with fear and grief at the loss of fathers and brothers; the dogs howled over their dead masters and the cattle were terrified with the scent of the blood of the murdered.

Yet was I there, all that long, dreadful night, with my dead and my wounded, and none but God as our physician and help.

"Oh my Heavenly Father, I cried, what shall I do? Thou seest my poor wounded boy and knowest my inexperience. Oh Heavenly Father, direct me what to do!"

And then I was directed as by a voice speaking to me.

The ashes of our fire was still smouldering. We had been burning the bark of the shag-bark hickory. I was directed to take those ashes and make a lye and put a cloth saturated with it right into the wound. It hurt, but little Alma was too near dead to heed it much. Again and again I saturated the cloth and put it into the hole from which the hip-joint had been ploughed, and each time mashed flesh and splinters of bone came away with the cloth; and the wound became as white as chicken's flesh.

Near by was a slippery-elm tree. From this I was told to make a slippery-elm poultice and fill the wound with it.

My eldest boy was sent to get the slippery-elm from the roots, the poultice was made, and the wound, which took fully a quarter of a yard of linen to cover, so large was it, was properly dressed.

It was then I found vent to my feelings in tears, and resigned myself to the anguish of the hour . . . .

I removed the wounded boy to a house, some distance off the next day, and dressed his hip; the Lord directing me as before. I was reminded that in my husband's trunk there was a bottle of balsam. This I poured into the wound, greatly soothing Alma's pain.

"Alma, my child!" I said, "you believe that the Lord made your hip?"

"Yes, mother."

"Well, the Lord can make something there in the place of your hip, don't you believe he can, Alma?"

"Do you think that the Lord can, mother?" inquired the child, in his simplicity.

"Yes, my son," I replied, "he has shown it all to me in a vision."

Then I laid him comfortably on his face, and said: "Now you lay like that, and don't move, and the Lord will make you another hip."

So Alma laid on his face for five weeks, until he was entirely recovered — a flexible gristle having grown in place of the missing joint and socket, which remains to this day a marvel to physicians.

On the day that he walked again I was out of the house fetching a bucket of water, when I heard screams from the children. Running back, in affright, I entered, and there was Alma on the floor, dancing around, and the children screaming in astonishment and joy.

It is now nearly forty years ago, but Alma has never been the least crippled during his life, and he has traveled quite a long period of the time as a missionary of the gospel and a living miracle of the power of God. [12]

Vision Of The Martyred David W. Patten

Wilford Woodruff, while on a mission to England, wrote
in his journal under the date of July 2nd, 1840, "I was informed
of a remarkable vision of Sister Ann Booth, which I have
written on the following page."

I, Ann Booth, wife of Robert Booth of the Town of Manchester, England, had the following vision on the 12th day of March in the year of our Lord 1840:

Being carried away in a vision to the place of departed souls, I saw twelve prisons, one above another, very large and built of solid stone. On arriving at the door of the uppermost prison, I beheld one of the twelve apostles of the Lamb, who had been martyred in America, standing at the door of the prison, holding a key with which he unlocked the door and went in.

I followed him. He appeared to be of a large size, thick set, with dark hair, dark eyes and eyebrows, of a smiling countenance, and on his head was a crown of gold or something brighter. He was dressed in a long, white robe, with the sleeves plaited from the shoulder to the hand. Upon his breast were four stars, apparently like gold, and a golden girdle about his loins. His feet were bare from above the ankles downward and his hands were also bare. As he entered the prison he seemed to stand about eight feet from the floor (which was of marble) as if the place was not worthy for him to stand upon. A very brilliant and glorious light surrounded him, while the rest of the prison was dark. But his light was peculiar to himself and did not reflect upon others who were in the prison, who were surrounded with a gloom of darkness.

On the right hand near the door stood John Wesley, who, on seeing the glorious personage, raised both hands and shouted, "Glory, honor, praise and power be ascribed unto God forever and forever — deliverance has come." The apostle then commenced to preach the baptism of repentance for remission of sins and the gift of the Holy Ghost by the laying on of hands, when the hundreds of prisoners gave a shout with a loud voice saying, "Glory be to God forever and ever." The marble floor was then removed and a river of water, clear as crystal, seemed to flow in its place.

The apostle then called to John Wesley by name, who came forward quickly, and both went down into the water, and he baptized him. Coming up out of the water, he laid hands on him for the gift of the Holy Ghost, at the same time ordaining him to the Priesthood of Aaron.

The apostle then retired to the place where he stood at first and John Wesley then proceded to baptize a man by the name of Killham, the leader of the New Connection of Methodists, and next John Madison, and then Scott and John Tongue. The three latter were Methodist preachers with whom I had formerly been acquainted. The next he baptized was my grandfather (Edmund Whitehead), and the next was my uncle (John Whitehead), and the next was my sister (Elizabeth Ottand), and next Joseph Lancashire, and next Samuel Robinson, and the next was my own mother. All these had lived and died Methodist, and I had been personally acquainted with them all.

And after this he baptized all the prisoners, amounting to many hundreds. After they were all baptized the apostle laid his hands on them and confirmed them every one. Then instantly the darkness dispersed and they were all surrounded and enveloped in a brilliant light such as surrounded the apostle at the first, and they all lifted their voices with one accord, giving glory to God for deliverance. My grandfather then came to me and blessed me, saying, "The Lord bless thee forever and ever."

I then awoke out of the vision, and felt so happy and overjoyed that I knew not how to remain in bed. But waking my husband, we arose; and taking the Bible, I opened providentially to the text of Isaiah, 24 — they shall be gathered together, etc. More and more astonished, I again opened the Bible to the first of St. John — the light shineth in darkness, etc. And again the third time I opened it and immediately cast my eyes upon the third chapter of Peter, 18, 19, 20 — speaking of the spirits in prison. Being before ignorant of these texts and opening upon each providentially, I was astonished beyond measure.

50

I would further state that at the time I had this vision I had never heard of the death of David W. Patten, whom I have since learned was one of the Twelve Apostles of the Latter-day Saints in America and was slain in the late persecution in the fall of 1838. But in the vision I knew it was an apostle who had been slain in America. Perhaps many will think lightly of this vision, but I hereby solemnly testify that I actually saw and heard in a vision what I have here related, and I give my name and set my seal in witness to the same, well knowing that I must stand before the judgment seat of Christ and answer for this testimony. [13]

"You Must Leave Home If You Join Those Mormons"

Conversion to the gospel was sometimes accompanied by
trials that required special comfort or direction. Many men
and women recount experiences similar to this one from
Caroline A. Joyce.

In the year 1842, I was living in the city of Boston, state of Massachusetts. One day I heard that a strange sect were preaching in Boylston Hall — they professed to believe in the same Gospel as taught by Jesus

Christ and ancient Apostles. I went to hear them. As we entered the hall they were singing a new song. The words were:

The Spirit of God like a fire is burning,
The Latter-day glory begins to come forth,
The visions and blessings of old are returning,
The angels are coming to visit the earth.

After the song a young man (Elder Erastus Snow) arose and took for his text these words: "And in the last days it shall come to pass that the Lord's House shall be established in the tops of the mountains and all nations shall flow unto it." He said the time for the fulfillment of this prophecy was near at hand; an angel had appeared unto a man named Joseph Smith, having the keys of the Everlasting Gospel to be preached to this generation, that those who obeyed it would gather out from the wicked, and prepare themselves for the coming of the Son of Man." He spoke of the great work already commenced in these last days, and while I listened, his words were like unto a song heard in my far off childhood, once forgotten but now returning afresh to my memory, and I cried for very joy. I went home to tell my father the good news, but my words returned to my own heart, for both my parents thought me insane, and talked to each other sadly of my condition and what to do with me. My heart was filled with sorrow and disappointment. I asked for the privilege of being baptized but was answered with these words by my father: "You must leave home if you join those Mormons." I went away and was baptized for the remission of my sins, but still with regret and an uncertainty as to the right to disobey my parents. Soon after, my father left the city, and my mother came and took me with her, to care for me, as she was fearful I would be "ruined by those deceivers."

One night I had been to meeting where the Spirit of God seemed to fill the house, and returned home thankful to my Heavenly Father that I ever heard the Gospel. I laid down to rest beside my mother, who commenced upbraiding me, and instantly I was filled with remorse that I was the cause of her unhappiness. I did not know what to say and was hesitating when, just over my head, a voice, not in a whisper, but still and low, said these words: "If you will leave father and mother, you shall have eternal life." I asked, "Mother, did you hear that?" She answered, "You are bewitched!" I knew then she had not heard the voice, but my mind was at rest and I went to sleep. I have heard the same voice since, not in dreams, but in daylight, when in trouble and uncertain which way to go; and I know God lives and guides this people called "Mormons." I know also the gifts and blessings are in the Church of Jesus Christ of Latter-day Saints, and that same faith once delivered to the Saints is also ours, if we live for it. [14]

51

The Mantle Falls On Brigham

One manifestation witnessed by an entire group of early
Saints was that in which the assurance came that Brigham Young
was the divinely approved successor to Joseph Smith. Here
it is related, along with her own testimony,
by Emmeline B. Wells, editor of the Woman's Exponent
and fifth president of the Relief Society.

I think this is the third fast day I have made up my mind that I certainly would speak, but did not because — well, there is always somebody ready to speak, and I guess I am not quick enough. I feel that I have a testimony to bear, that I have always kept from the very day that I entered the City of Nauvoo and saw the Prophet Joseph. He came down to the boat to meet the saints who were coming from the eastern states and the middle states up to the west.

I had been baptized by the wish of my mother, who became a Latter-day Saint as soon as she heard the gospel, but I had no testimony and I had not very much faith, because I did not know much about things. I was always interested in the people that were scholarly and in the greatest schools of the world, and I was particularly happy to believe that I was going to be very great and prominent.

When I came up the river on the boat, and standing on the top of the boat to see the Prophet on the landing from the boat, I knew instantly then that the gospel was true by the feeling that pervaded me from the crown of my head to the end of my fingers and toes, and every part of my body. I was sure then that I was right, that "Mormonism" was true and that I was fully paid for all the sacrifices that I had made to come to Nauvoo. I felt that just to see him would be worth it all. I had been prepared in a measure for seeing him, but I want to tell you I was not disappointed, because there never was a man like him.

The only incident where a man resembled him was when Brigham Young announced himself as president of the Church and the successor of the Prophet Joseph. I don't remember the words, but that was the announcement that he made in the grove on Temple Hill in the City of Nauvoo. There were but very few people that knew he had come. They knew all the Twelve were away at the time that the Prophet Joseph and his brother, Hyrum, were slain, and I think very few in that audience knew that Brigham Young had returned. When he came forward and made that announcement, the whole company arose and exclaimed, in one voice, you might say, that it was the Prophet Joseph.

I was standing in a wagon box on wheels, so I did not have to rise, but those who were seated arose and made that exclamation. I could see very well, and every one of them thought it was really the Prophet Joseph risen from the dead. But after Brigham Young had spoken a few words, the tumult subsided, and the people really knew that it was not the Prophet Joseph, but the President of the quorum of the Twelve Apostles. It was the most wonderful manifestation, I think, that I have ever known or seen, and I have seen a very great number. [16]

Eliza Receives A Visitation From Joseph

Eliza R. Snow was sealed to the Prophet Joseph on June 29th,
1842. Their relationship indeed continued beyond the grave,
as attested to by Assistant Church Historian Andrew Jenson.

After the martyrdom of her husband, June 27, 1844, Sister Eliza
was prostrated with grief, and besought the Lord with all the fervency
of her soul to permit her to follow the Prophet at once, and not leave
her in so dark and wicked a world. And so set was her mind on the
matter, that she did not and could not cease that prayer of her heart
until the Prophet came to her and told her that she must not continue
to supplicate the Lord in that way, for her petition was not in accordance
with his design concerning her. Joseph told her that his work upon
earth was completed as far as the mortal tabernacle was concerned,
but her's was not; the Lord desired her, and so did her husband, to
live many years, and assist in carrying on the great Latter-day work
which Joseph had been chosen to establish. That she must be of good
courage and help to cheer, and lighten the burdens of others. And
that she must turn her thoughts away from her own loneliness, and
seek to console her people in their bereavement and sorrow. [15]

A Husband Returns To Comfort His Wife

Upon the death of her husband Newel, Lydia Knight was left
alone in Indian country. Even while dying he promised her,
"I will not leave you."

Time was empty of incident or interest to Lydia until the 4th of
February, when Brother Miller, who had been to Winter Quarters for
provisions, returned, and brought tidings of a revelation showing the
order of the organization of the camp of the Saints, and also the joyful
news that Brothers E. T. Benson and Erastus Snow were coming soon
to Ponca to organize the Saints according to the pattern given in the
revelation.

On the day of the organization, Lydia returned from the meeting
and sat down in her home full of sad thoughts. How could she, who
had never taken any care except that which falls to every woman's
share, prepare herself and family to return to Winter Quarters and from
thence take a journey of a thousand miles into the Rocky Mountains.
The burden weighed her very spirit down until she cried out in her
pain: "Oh Newel, why hast thou left me!"

As she spoke, he stood by her side, with a lovely smile on his face,
and said: "Be calm, let not sorrow overcome you. It was necessary
that I should go. I was needed behind the veil to represent the true
condition of this camp and people. You cannot fully comprehend it

now; but the time will come when you shall know why I left you and our little ones. Therefore, dry up your tears. Be patient, I will go before you and protect you in your journeyings. And you and your little ones shall never perish for lack of food. Although the ravens of the valley should feed you and your little ones you shall not perish for the want of bread."

As he spoke the last words, she turned, and there appeared three ravens. Turning again to where her husband had stood, he was not.

This was a great comfort and help to her, and her spirits were revived and strengthened by the promises made. [17]

A Mother's Prayer Answered

President Joseph F. Smith once said, "I love to hear a woman pray. They can approach nearer to the Lord than men can, as a general thing; or my mother did." [18] Here he relates one incident in the life of Mary Fielding Smith that doubtlessly helped him to feel that way.

In the spring of 1847 a portion of our family crossed the plains, following the pioneers to the valley of the Great Salt Lake, the remainder of the family intending to proceed on their journey to the west in the following spring.

In the fall of 1847, my mother and her brother, Joseph Fielding, made a trip down the Missouri river to St. Joseph, Mo., about fifty miles, for the purpose of obtaining provisions and clothing for the family for the coming winter, and for the journey across the plains the following spring. They took two wagons with two yokes of oxen on each. I was almost nine years of age at this time, and accompanied my mother and uncle on this journey as a teamster. The weather was unpropitious, the roads were bad, and it rained a great deal during the journey, so that the trip was a very hard, trying and unpleasant one. At St. Joseph we purchased our groceries and dry goods, and at Savannah we laid in our store of flour, meal, corn, bacon and other provisions.

Returning to Winter Quarters, we camped one evening in an open prairie on the Missouri river bottoms, by the side of a small spring creek, which emptied into the river about three-quarters of a mile from us. We were in plain sight of the river, and could apparently see over every foot of the little open prairie where we were camped, to the river on the southwest, to the bluffs on the northeast, and to the timber which skirted the prairie on the right and left. Camping near by, on the other side of the creek, were some men with a herd of beef cattle, which they were driving to Savannah and St. Joseph for market. We usually unyoked our oxen and turned them loose to feed during our encampments at night, but this time, on account of the proximity of this herd of cattle, fearing that they might get mixed up and driven off with them, we turned our oxen out to feed in their yokes. Next morning when we came to look them up, to our great disappointment our best yoke of oxen was not to be found.

Uncle Fielding and I spent all the morning, well nigh until noon, hunting for them but without avail. The grass was tall, and in the morning was wet with heavy dew. Tramping through this grass and through the woods and over the bluffs, we were soaked to the skin, fatigued, disheartened and almost exhausted. In this pitiable plight I was the first to return to our wagons, and as I approached I saw my mother kneeling down in prayer. I halted for a moment and then drew gently near enough to hear her pleading with the Lord not to suffer us to be left in this helpless condition, but to lead us to recover our lost team, that we might continue our travels in safety. When she arose from her knees I was standing near by. The first expression I caught upon her precious face was a lovely smile, which, discouraged as I was, gave me renewed hope and an assurance I had not felt before.

A few moments later Uncle Fielding came to the camp, wet with the dews, faint, fatigued and thoroughly disheartened. His first words were: "Well, Mary, the cattle are gone!"

Mother replied in a voice which fairly rang with cheerfulness, "Never mind, your breakfast has been waiting for hours, and now, while you and Joseph are eating, I will just take a walk out and see if I can find the cattle."

My uncle held up his hands in blank astonishment, and if the Missouri river had suddenly turned to run up stream, neither of us could have been much more surprised. "Why, Mary," he exclaimed, "What do you mean? We have been all over this country, all through the timber and through the herd of cattle, and our oxen are gone — they are not to be found. I believe they have been driven off, and it is useless for you to attempt to do such a thing as to hunt for them."

"Never mind me," said mother, "get your breakfast and I will see," and she started toward the river, following down the river, and she had hardly got out of speaking distance, when the man in charge of the herd of beef cattle rode up from the opposite side of the creek and called out: "Madam, I saw your oxen over in that direction this morning about daybreak," pointing in the opposite direction from that in which mother was going. We heard plainly what he said, but mother went right on, paid no attention to his remark and did not even turn her head to look at him. A moment later the man rode off rapidly toward his herd, which had been gathered in the opening near the edge of the woods, and they were soon under full drive for the road leading toward Savannah, and soon disappeared from view.

My mother continued straight down the little stream of water, until she stood almost on the bank of the river, and then she beckoned to us. (I was watching her every moment and was determined that she should not get out of my sight.) Instantly we rose from the "mess-chest" on which our breakfast had been served, and started toward her, and, like John, who outran the other disciple to the sepulchre, I outran my uncle and came first to the spot where my mother stood.

There I saw our oxen fastened to a clump of willows growing in the botton of a deep gulch which had been washed out of the sandy banks of the river by the little spring creek, perfectly concealed from view. We were not long in releasing them from bondage and getting back to our camp, where the other cattle had been fastened to the wagon wheels all the morning, and we were soon on our way homeward bound, rejoicing.

This circumstance was one of the first practical and positive demonstrations of the efficacy of prayer I had ever witnessed. It made an indelible impression upon my mind, and has been a source of comfort, assurance and guidance to me throughout all my life. [19]

Sister Wilcox Shares In A Vision Of Heber C. Kimball

*Heber C. Kimball was a visionary mcn, and on several occasions
made prophecies regarding what would befall the Saints.
Sister Amanda H. Wilcox both heard him describe and saw a
portion of a vision that Brother Kimball was given. Only the first
part of her account of that experience is reprinted here.*

During the latter part of May, 1868, President Heber C. Kimball and I were standing in front of his place, on North Main. After a few moments' conversation he turned to me and said, "Now, Sister Amanda, I am going to tell you something." Looking south, he observed, "What do you see?" I told him that I did not know any of the places on Main street except Brother Wells', Bishop Hunter's, William Jennings', Walker Brothers' and the Tithing Office. He then remarked, "I will begin with Brother Wells' place. It will be torn down and a six-story building will be erected on that corner. All of the houses south of that place will be removed to make room for buildings that will average from three to six stories high.

"Now we will come back from Fourth South to the Council House corner. Here a large fireproof building will be erected with an addition to it on the west. Where the Tithing Office now stands will be constructed a building that will be a credit and honor to the inhabitants of this whole intermountain region. The land around the Temple Block will be owned by the Saints and this will become a city of beautiful buildings.

"Next comes the Temple. What do you expect to see there?" I told him that I expected to see the Savior, Joseph, Hyrum and others. He said, "Have you seen the Temple picture?" I said that I had not. He then put his hand on my shoulder and said, "Now look." "Oh, how white and beautiful," I exclaimed. He then removed his hand and the vision was gone. [20]

"I Knew The Comforter Was There"

Aurelia Spencer Rogers was the woman who suggested the
organization that became the Primary and served as its
first president in 1878. In her Life Sketches *she tells of*
a number of spiritual experiences, both in her Church work and
in her personal life.

My next child after Lucy, a little girl, died when three months old
of whooping cough. The winter following, my health was worse than
usual, and in the spring I passed through an ordeal that I think well
to mention. The measles had broken out again in Farmington, and proved
fatal to many. At that time I had a desire to go to the city and visit
my sisters, and not being able to do much work at home, it was thought
the change might do me good: so I went. After stopping in the city
nearly two weeks, the time drew near for me to go home but I was
not able to go, having been prostrated with those old distressed spells.

About this time Lucy, the only child I had with me, came down
with measles. It seemed she must have been exposed before leaving
home; scarlet-fever set in which endangered her life. When the disease
was at its height, Ellen's baby, Ivy, also came down with measles. I
was the cause of all this trouble; I had brought sickness to my sister's
family and could not even wait on myself or little girl. This wore on
me until I was almost beside myself with grief; my mind became diseased,
and I experienced the most horrible feelings imaginable. One night they
thought Ivy was going to die, and if I ever prayed fervently to the
Lord, it was then, that He would spare the lives of our children; but
if either child was to be taken it might be mine. I could not endure
the thought of my sister losing her babe, for she had already buried
four children.

While in the midst of this anxiety, lying on my bed, wondering
if the Lord had indeed forsaken us, all at once a change came over
me; everything seemed so lovely and beautiful, and I was as happy
as could be for a few minutes. I saw no person, heard no voice, yet
knew the Comforter was there, and accepted it as such, feeling to thank
the Lord for even a glimmer of light.

The children were both spared. [21]

57

Revelation To The Mother Of An Unborn Apostle

The life of Apostle Melvin J. Ballard had an unusual beginning.
It is here related by his sister, Myrtle Shurtliff.

Melvin Joseph Ballard was a child of promise. He was carried beneath
his mother's heart during a period of poverty, of depression, of crop
failure, and of sorrow. She had given birth to six children. Two were
taken in death while in the first year of their lives, just ten days apart.

They were twins, a boy and a girl. Sorrow and sickness had weakened her physical strength, and in the years to follow she lost several children who were born prematurely. Her heart was sore; her arms were empty; and again the life of her unborn child was threatened. Many days and weeks she was bedfast, but like Rachel of old, her heart yearned for a child, and she cried unto the Lord, "Give me children, else I die."

Her husband had taken the children a block away to see a parade, and while he was gone, she raised her trembling body from the bed and crawled and locked the door so that she might pour out her soul to God on her knees in prayer. She called to remembrance her willingness to bear children, her approval of her husband's marriage to her sister, that a greater posterity might build up his kingdom in Zion. She supplicated the Lord for help. She felt that she had done all that was in her power, and she asked to know her standing in his sight.

God hearkened unto her prayer, and a comfort was given to her. She saw no person, but a voice spoke plainly to her saying, "Be of good cheer. Your life is acceptable, and you will bear a son who will become an apostle of the Lord, Jesus Christ."

In due time her child was born. She did bear a son, her last son, and he was named Melvin Joseph. His life was precious in the sight of his father and mother, and they recognized in him a choice spirit. He was also honored by his brothers and sisters, although they did not know of the promise given him. [22]

58

The English Newspaper In America Four Days Off The Press

To further genealogy and temple work appears to be a frequent reason for divine assistance. Margaret Ballard, mother of Melvin J. Ballard, tells of a remarkable incident that occurred in their family, an incident in which her daughter played a major part.

On the 17th of May, 1884, the Logan Temple was dedicated. The second day after the dedication President John Taylor said that all members of the Church who were worthy, and who desired to go through the temple, might do so the next day. My husband being a bishop, was very busy writing out recommends to all who wished to go through the temple, when my daughter, Ellen, came in and asked for her father.

I told her that her father was busy and asked her to give the newspaper, which she had in her hand, to me so that I might give it to him.

She said: "No, the man who gave the paper to me told me to give it to no one but Father."

I let the child take the paper to her father, and when he looked it over, he was greatly surprised for he saw that the paper had been printed in Berkshire, England, his birthplace, and was only four days from the press. He was so amazed at such an incident that he called Ellen and asked her where the man was who had given her the paper.

She said that she was playing on the sidewalk with other children when two men came down the street walking in the middle of the road. One of them called to her, saying: "Come here, little girl." She hesitated at first, for there were other little girls with her. Then he pointed to her and said: "You." She went out, and he gave her the paper and told her to give it to her father.

This paper contained about sixty names of the dead acquaintances of my husband, giving the dates of their birth and death. My husband was baptized for the men, and I for the women, and all the work was done for them. Again I felt the Lord was mindful of us in blessing us abundantly. [23]

A Manifestation Regarding Temple Work

Another sister whose efforts in genealogy were thus aided
was Lorena E. Washburn Larsen. The experience is related by
her son Enoch.

She very often would sit up late at night working for genealogy. Sometimes it would be two o'clock in the morning before she would get all of a certain line put down on the family group sheets before she could go to bed.

One night after she had gone to bed and was asleep she was awakened very suddenly — there by her bed stood two women. One of the women spoke to Mother and said, "I am not a blood relative of yours, but I married one of your relatives. You will find my name in a Washburn book in the Manti Temple on page 54 about half way down the page." Then she gave her name. The two women disappeared.

Mother thought about this for a little while and then went back to sleep. A little while later Mother was awakened again and the same thing was repeated. After the two women had disappeared, Mother got out of bed and went down stairs and wrote all the details down on paper. Mother said she was sure it was a mistake because she had searched every Washburn book in the Manti Temple and there was not such a book there like the one the lady had described.

About a month later, Mother went to the Manti Temple. Peter Poulson was the chief recorder there. Mother approached Bro. Poulson and asked if she could see this certain Washburn book (which she knew was not there, and so Bro. Poulson would say there was no such book there).

Bro. Poulson said, "O.K. Sis. Larsen — I was searching in the vault a week ago and I came to this Washburn book, and I thought you would like to see it, so I laid it aside for you when you came again." He got the book and handed it to Mother. She was still doubtful as she turned to page 54. To her surprise, there she found it all as the woman had told Mother, and as she had written it down. [24]

A Dream Of Waiting Children

Lorena E. Larsen also experienced a number of helpful dreams that she considered to have great significance.

In 1897 I was so sorely tried; my husband was not able to provide for his family and our children had to go without things to make them comfortable, and many things were trying me. I felt that although I struggled to provide to the best of my ability, it was not sufficient, and I felt that my husband, though such a splendid man, yet was partial in his dealings with his families, and that he was unsympathetic with my part of the family. I became discouraged.

To rear my family practically alone was a sore trial.

And so I decided that I would have no more children unless my husband could come and live with us as a father should live with his family, and give us the love and sympathy which every family should have. I was really rebellious about having any more children under the present circumstances.

One night I dreamed that I passed out of the body, and was surprised to find that there wasn't a greater change between this life and the life hereafter.

I looked at my body lying on the bed and I fully realized that I was really in the Spirit World.

Immediately my whole life passed before my mind like a panorama, and I had a knowledge of what the Lord approved of, and what he did not approve. I was surprised to find that some of my human weaknesses which I myself had condemned, were of little or no consequence. The only thing that was held against me was the rebellious feeling I had about having more children.

I there and then knew that before I came to earth I had promised to be the mother to a certain number of children, and there were two or three of that number that were still unborn. I knew exactly the number then, but after I came to myself again I could not remember definitely.

When the realization of the fact came upon me that I had failed to keep my promise with the Lord, had failed to fill the measure of my creation, I was in hell. The torment of my mind was past description. I wrung my hands in awful agony. I looked at my body on the bed, my spiritual hand took hold of my mortal hand, and I said, if I had only known, if I had only known. I wondered how long this torment of soul would last, and immediately I knew it would never end. I looked in every direction, I could see there was no end to time and space. The walls of the house did not obstruct the view. In a northwesterly direction from where I stood I saw a man afar off, coming through the air toward me. He was small at first, but increased in size as he came nearer. I knew when I first saw him that he was a good man, and that when he came I could tell him everything.

Presently he stood beside me and I told him my story. I said it was not because I did not want more children, but because they were not properly cared for. He said, "Don't you know that was a trick of the adversary to cut you short of your glory?" I knew as I stood there that he spoke the truth, and as I wrung my hands I said, "I know, I know."

I then asked him, "Is there no way that I can get back into my body and fill the measure of my creation?" He said, "Only by faith and much prayer." I said, "Faith is a gift of God, but I will pray."

I got down on my knees and began to pray earnestly, and the next thing I knew I awoke, and there was a tingling sensation all through my body, like when a leg or arm goes to sleep. I got up and knelt by the side of my bed, and offered such a prayer of praise and thanksgiving to the Lord as I had never offered before, and I promised the Lord I would publish my experience as far as possible, so that no other woman should have such an awful experience when passing to the Spirit World. It seemed to me that it was hell of the worst type.

I have had two children since that time, but have never been sure that there was not another one that I should have had.

The Lord has been so good to me. He has rewarded me in the quality of my children a thousand fold, for the trials I have passed through. [25]

"Chosen Of The Lord"

Susa Young Gates, a daughter of Brigham Young and
Lucy Bigelow Young, received, along with others, a special
witness to the divine calling of President Joseph F. Smith.

The early days of April in the year 1893 were heavy with storm and gloom. A leaden sky stretched over the earth; every day the rain beat down upon it, and the storm-winds swept over it with terrific force. Yet the brightness and the glory of those days far outshone the gloom. It was during those tempestuous days of early April that the Salt Lake Temple was dedicated.

During the dedicatory services, it was my privilege to transcribe the official notes of the various meetings. At the first service, which was known as the "official dedication," I was sitting on the lower side of the east pulpits, at the recorder's table. Brother John Nicholson, who had been busy at the outer gate, came in and sat down beside me, just as President Joseph F. Smith arose to speak. Almost as soon as President Smith began to address the Saints, there shone through his countenance a radiant light that gave me a peculiar feeling. I thought that the clouds must have lifted, and that a stream of sunlight had lighted on the President's head.

I turned to Brother Nicholson and whispered: "What a singular effect of sunlight on the face of President Smith! Do look at it."

He whispered back: "There is no sunlight outdoors — nothing but dark clouds and gloom."

I looked out of the window, and somewhat to my surprise, I saw that Brother Nicholson had spoken the truth. There was not the slightest rift in the heavy, black clouds above the city; there was not a gleam of sunshine anywhere. Whence, then, came the light that still shone from the face of President Smith?

Most people remember the terrible storm of that day. It was a day not easily to be forgotten. I was told afterwards by Sister Edna Smith, who lived on the corner of First West and North Temple Streets, that her parents came outside of their door at about the time of the opening of the services. They stood for some time watching the gloomy, cloud-swept heavens intently, when they saw all at once a glow of glorious light surround the Temple and circle about it as if it were an intelligible Presence. Later also, my sister, Carlie Young Cannon, who lived outside of the city, on what is known as the Cannon Farm, informed me that some members of her family came outside of their door on this same stormy morning. As they stood looking up toward the city, they, too, saw the strange light circling about the Temple wall. From their point of vantage they could see clearly that it was no effect of sunshine; for the clouds did not lift for an instant that day.

Whence, then, came the light that shone from the face of President Smith? I was sure that I had seen the actual Presence of the Holy Spirit, focused upon the features of the beloved leader and prophet, Joseph F. Smith. It was but an added testimony to me that he was the "Chosen of the Lord." I cherish the occurrence as one of the most sacred experiences of my life. [26]

62

The Lord Speaks To A Twelve-Year-Old Girl

Many women in the acquaintance of Heber J. Grant participated in unusual spiritual experiences. In this story he tells of a revelation given to his young daughter upon her mother's death.

About one hour before my wife died, I called my children into her room and told them that their mother was dying and for them to bid her good-bye. One of the little girls, about twelve years of age, said to me: "Papa, I do not want my mama to die. I have been with her in the hospital in San Francisco for six months. Time and time again when mama was in distress, you have administered to her, and she has been relieved of her pain and quietly gone to sleep. I want you to lay hands upon my mama and heal her."

I told my little girl that we all had to die sometime, and that I felt assured in my heart that her mother's time had arrived. She and the rest of the children left the room.

I then knelt down by the bed of my wife (who by this time had lost consciousness) and I told the Lord I acknowledged His hand in life, in death, in joy, in sorrow, in prosperity, or adversity. I thanked Him for the knowledge I had that my wife belonged to me for all eternity, that through the power and authority of the priesthood here on the earth that I could and would have my wife forever if I were only faithful as she had been. But I told the Lord that I lacked the strength to have my wife die and have it affect the faith of my little children in the ordinances of the Gospel of Jesus Christ; and I supplicated the Lord with all the strength that I possessed that He would give to that little girl of mine a knowledge that it was His mind and His will that her mama should die.

Within an hour my wife passed away, and I called the children back into the room. My little boy, about five and one-half or six years of age, was weeping bitterly, and the little girl twelve years of age took him in her arms and said: "Do not weep, Heber; since we went out of this room, the voice of the Lord from Heaven has said to me, in the death of mama, the will of the Lord shall be done."[27]

63

A Warning Concerning Revelation

Any man or woman in the Church who receives a spiritual prompting contrary to the revelations given through proper priesthood channels is well-advised to examine the source of that prompting. Newel Knight relates an incident in which a sister overstepped the bounds of her authority.

Brother Joseph from time to time sent copies of revelations to me for the benefit of the branch over which I presided in common with all the Saints in Zion. On reading one of these revelations to the branch, my aunt of whom mention has been made, arose and contradicted the revelation, saying it must be taken in a spiritual light. She went to such a length that I felt constrained to rebuke her by the authority of the Priesthood. At this she was angry, and from that time sought to influence all who would listen to her. The result was a division of feeling in the branch, and her husband partook of her spirit until he became so enthusiastic, that he went from branch to branch crying, "hosanna, glory to God! Zion is redeemed! and blessed is he that bringeth good tidings to the people!" Sister Peck at length began to feel the weight of what she had done, but she could not recall it. She seemed racked with great torment, her mind found no rest, until a burning fever brought her to a sick bed. She sent for several of the Elders to administer to her, but found no relief. At last she sent for

P. P. Pratt, Lyman Wight and myself, we laid our hands upon her and administered to her, after which she looked up in despair and said she hoped I would deliver her from the awful state she was in. Her whole frame was racked with intense anguish while her mind seemed almost in despair. Brother Parley said to me: "Brother Newel, you must do something for her." My soul was drawn out in pity for her, yet I knew not what to do. I felt impressed to call the branch together that evening.

When the meeting had been opened as usual, I arose not knowing what to do or what to say. After requesting the prayers and united faith of all present, the Spirit of the Lord came upon me, so that I was able to make plain the cause of Sister Peck's illness — that she had risen up in opposition to the Priesthood which had been placed over that branch of the Church, and contradicted the revelations of God, and that by the sympathies shown her, a division of feeling had gained advantage over them, until Sister Peck had fallen completely under the power of Satan, and could not extricate herself. I told the brethren and sisters, if they would repent of what they had done, and renew their covenants one with another and with the Lord, and uphold the authorities placed over them, and also the revelations which the Lord had given unto us, it would be all right with Sister Peck, for this would break the bands of Satan and make us free.

64

I had no sooner closed my remarks than with one united voice, all came forward and agreed to do so. I then went to Sister Peck, and in the name of Jesus Christ, and by virtue of the Holy Priesthood, commanded the evil powers to depart from her, and blessed her with peace and strength, both of body and mind. I then dismissed the meeting and told the family to go to bed, and rest as usual, and all would be well. Early the next morning I called to see her, she stretched out her hand as soon as she saw me, and said, O, Brother Newel, forgive me! I did not believe one word you said last night, but when I awoke this morning I found I was not in hell. Her rejoicings were very great, and union again prevailed with us, and we all felt we had learned a lesson that would be of lasting benefit to us. [28]

To touch
Where life is leaving,
Hands charged with faith,
To bless,
And then —
To feel the certain flow
Of life again —

Chapter Five

THE GIFT OF FAITH TO HEAL

Among the ordinances definitely assigned to the priesthood is the ordinance of administering to the sick. The general rule is quite clear: "Is any sick among you? Let him call for the elders of the church; and let them pray over him, anointing him with oil in the name of the Lord."[1]

Additional information from the prophets, however, has made it clear that women have a significant part to play, if they will, in the spiritual processes of healing the sick. This may be done as they add their faith and prayers to those of the priesthood brethren, or in circumstances that require their acting independently.

From the earliest days of the restored Church, women were given to understand that they had this privilege. In a blessing given in 1837 to Sister Eda Rogers by Joseph Smith Sr., father of the Prophet, she was instructed:

> In the absence of thy husband thou must pray with thy family. When they are sick thou shalt lay hands on them, and they shall recover. Sickness shall stand back.[2]

Many of the sisters did accept this privilege and use it to great benefit. Some of the brethren, however, did not feel that it was appropriate for women to bless the sick. Complaint came to Joseph Smith that women had administered to the sick "by the prayer of faith, the laying on of hands, or the anointing with oil." After discussing the matter, Joseph replied:

> Who are better qualified to administer than our faithful and zealous sisters, whose hearts are full of faith, tenderness, sympathy and compassion. No one.[3]

Emmeline B. Wells, in telling of her first acquaintance with women administering in Nauvoo, said that

> when she first went there, she was taken sick. Mother Whitney sent for "Aunt" Jane Young, wife of Uncle Joseph Young, who poured the oil on her head and then she, Mother Whitney herself, sealed it upon her head. Afterwards in explaining this to the young convert, Mother Whitney told her (Aunt Em) that the Prophet had given women this privilege. [4]

A number of sisters evidently were set apart for such administrations. Elizabeth Whitney, in *The Woman's Exponent*, says:

> I was also ordained and set apart under the hand of Joseph Smith the Prophet to administer to the sick and comfort the sorrowful. Several other sisters were also ordained and set apart to administer in these holy ordinances. [5]

After the Church moved to Utah, the sisters continued to receive encouragement to use their spiritual powers toward healing. Two statements of Brigham Young make this evident.

> It is the privilege of a mother to have faith and to administer to her child; this she can do herself, as well as sending for the elders to have the benefit of their faith. [6]

> I want a wife that can take care of my children when I am away, who can pray, lay on hands, anoint with oil, and baffle the enemy; and this is a spiritual wife. [7]

The sisters were exhorted to this duty by other of the Church leaders as well. President Zina D. H. Young told the sisters of the Relief Society of a meeting she had attended. "Bishop Whitney spoke beautifully of mothers administering; what it would save the Elders; I wish you could all have heard him." [8]

At the Relief Society Jubilee in the Tabernacle, March 17, 1892, President Joseph F. Smith said:

> In relation to laying on of hands by sisters . . . it is the proper thing for mothers, who have received their blessings in the house of God, to pray for their sick and to rebuke diseases. It is just as much the right of the mother as of the father, although he, holding the priesthood, can do it by virtue of this, as well as in the name of the Lord. The women are not especially called upon to visit from house to house to administer to the sick, but they can do so properly, if called upon. [9]

Years later, President Joseph F. Smith, in the "Questions and Answers" section of *The Improvement Era*, gave some further light on this subject.

> Does a wife hold the priesthood in connection with her husband? and may she lay hands on the sick with him, with authority?

> A wife does not hold the priesthood in connection with her husband, but she enjoys the benefits thereof with him; and if she is requested to lay hands on the sick with him, or with any other officer holding

the Melchizedek priesthood, she may do so with perfect propriety. It is no uncommon thing for a man and wife unitedly to administer to their children, and the husband being mouth, he may properly say out of courtesy, "By authority of the holy priesthood in us vested." [10]

With that encouragement and those guidelines provided by the leadership of the Church, the sisters of last century exercised on innumerable occasions the gift of "faith to heal."

As policies have evolved since the earliest days of the Church, responsibilities of the priesthood have become more clarified. To "call for the elders of the church" is still the proper response when sickness comes. For a husband or father to join with a home teacher or other trusted bearer of the priesthood in bringing a healing blessing to the home is a beautiful, obedient, orderly means of using ordained authority.

But the sisters have a right and an obligation to know that in addition to calling upon the priesthood, or as they may by circumstances be forced to act independently, they are not impotent. As moved upon by the Spirit, they may — not through assumption of priesthood authority, but through the powers of faith upon which all things are based — seek and obtain a healing blessing from the Lord.

The experiences of our sisters in the early days of the Church should inspire us to this end.

Emma and Counselors Administer

Emma Smith, wife of the Prophet Joseph and first president of the Relief Society, was a lady of amazing strengths. Oliver Cowdery, an intimate friend to the Smiths, wrote of her, "I can say in justice her character stands as fair for morality, piety, and virtue, as any in the world." [11] Here is one incident, recorded in the minutes of the Nauvoo Relief Society for April 19, 1842, in which Emma and her counselors evidenced their spiritual powers.

Mrs. Durfee bore testimony to the great blessing she received when administered to after the close of the last meeting, by Emma Smith and Counselors Cleveland and Whitney. She said she never realized more benefit through any administration — that she was healed and thought the sisters had more faith than the brethren. [12]

An Angel Gives Instructions For Healing

Sarah S. Leavitt, in her journal, relates several divine
manifestations. The most remarkable occurred when she and
her husband were living ten miles from Kirtland. They were trying
to remain in the good graces of their neighbors in spite of
being Mormons, but were finding it difficult. A girl named
Louisa, who was living with them, fell ill. The neighbors were insisting
that a doctor be called, and were threatening to take away the
Leavitt's team to pay for the doctor. Sarah thought that
Louisa had already taken too much medicine.

I lay pondering on our situation, thinking we should be undone
if our team was took from us, and prayed earnestly to the Lord to
let us know what we should do. There was an angel stood by my bed
to answer my prayer. He told me to call Louisa up and lay my hands
upon her head in the name of Jesus Christ and administer to her and
she should recover. I awakened my husband, who lay by my side,
and told him to get up, make a fire, and get Louisa up. She would
hear to him sooner than to me; to tell her that an angel had told me
to lay my hands upon her head in the name of the Lord Jesus Christ
and administer to her in His name and she should recover. She was
perfectly ignorant of Mormonism; all she had ever heard about it was
in Kirtland, what few days we stayed there and what we had told
her. Her mind was weak, indeed, but she got up and I administered
to her in faith, having the gift from the Lord. It was about midnight
when this was done and she began to recover from that time and was
soon up and about, and the honor, praise and glory be to God and
the Lamb. So you see, our enemies were defeated of their plan, but
knew nothing of the cause of her recovery. [13]

68

An English Sister Healed In Nauvoo

Another of the early women, Abigail Leonard, tells of an
incident in which healing came under the hands of the sisters.

As soon as we were located [Nauvoo], we were all seized with
sickness, and scarcely had I recovered, when there came into our midst
some brethren from England, who were homeless, and our people took
them in with their own families. One of the families we took to live
with us. The woman was sick . . . . The sisters came, washed, anointed,
and administered to her. The patient's extremities were cold, her eyes
set, a spot in the back apparently mortified, and every indication that
death was upon her. But before the sisters had ceased to administer,
the blood went coursing through her system, and to her extremities,
and she was sensibly better. Before night her appetite returned . . . .
In three days she sat up and had her hair combed, and soon recovered. [14]

"The Devil Shall Not Have Power Thus To Afflict Me!"

*While Addison Pratt was away on a mission, his wife Louisa
was alone with four children in Nauvoo.*

Another circumstance transpired in which I saw the mercy of God
manifested towards me in a peculiar manner. My brother-in-law, J.
Crosby, went on a mission to the States, returned with the small-pox.
I took my four children and went to see him, not knowing the character
of his disease. My two youngest children had not been vaccinated.
I went to his bedside; he told me I had better go out, as there was
reason to fear his disease was contagious. The news spread rapidly
that we had been exposed to the small pox! The nieghbors were all
alarmed; dared not come to my house.

In nine days from the time, my third daughter began to have a
fever. I sent for the Elders to administer; they were afraid to come.
"The devil," said I, "shall not have power thus to afflict me!" I then
laid hands on my child, and rebuked the fever. Eleven little pimples
came out but never filled. In a few days the fever was gone. I showed
the child to one acquainted with that disease; he said that it was an
attack; that I had conquered it by faith. I thanked the Lord while I
realized what a determined will may accomplish with a firm trust in
God. [15]

69

The Healing Of George Patten

*Charles C. Rich and his wife Sarah passed through many
adventures that are detailed by their biographer, John Henry
Evans. This incident illustrates the determination and
faith of Sarah.*

At Garden Grove, which the family reached in the latter part of
April, they were delayed by the illness of George Patten, whom they
were taking west with them. George was then in his eighteenth year.
Born in Pennsylvania, he was left motherless at seven. Then for a time
he had been placed with some relatives in Philadelphia, who had grossly
neglected him. Later, when his father had taken him home again, he
had gone to Nauvoo. Here he was baptized in the Mississippi river,
into the Mormon Church.

Says Patten, in a short sketch of himself, written when he was an
old man: "On March 6 we broke camp ... d moved slowly, on account
of the weather, on Shariton river, some sixty miles from Nauvoo. I
took down sick and had to lie rocking about in the wagon for three
weeks. When we got to Garden Grove my hip bones were clear through
the flesh, and people thought I must die. But President Young blessed

me and said I should live. By the kindness of Brother and Sister Rich, and the blessings of the Lord I was spared."

Sarah Pea-Rich, however, gives us some interesting details in connection with this sickness. Arriving at the Grove, young Patten was put to bed in a tent, where he was expected to die any moment. General Rich and another man took turns sitting up with him. One night, says Mrs. Rich, the General woke her with the request that she take his place at the bedside of the boy, while he snatched a few minutes' sleep and rest.

On going into the tent, she looked at George. He lay stretched on the couch, all but dead. His breathing was heavy and his lips very much swollen. Taking her seat beside the bed, she pondered over the situation. What would she do if George were her own flesh and blood? She knelt down and prayed — not that God would heal the boy, but that He would show her what to do under the circumstances.

> When I got up from praying [she tells us] I was led by my feelings to put a teaspoonful of consecrated oil in his mouth. His tongue was drawn far back in his mouth and was very black, and his eyes, to all appearance, set in his head. I did not see that he swallowed the oil. I anointed his face and head with oil, asking the Lord meanwhile to bless the same. Then, in a little while, I gave him another teaspoonful of oil. To my great joy I noticed that he swallowed it. With a soft swab I rubbed his tongue and mouth, in order to remove the black crust that was forming in his mouth and throat. I then gave him a little brandy and water, and he swallowed that. Then I made some tea of what we called horse-mint, which he also swallowed. After that I washed his hands and face in water and soda. Thus I worked with the dear boy till daylight.

> To my great joy George opened his eyes and looked at me as though he were astonished. I said, "George, do you know me?" And he answered in a whisper, "Yes!"

At dawn Mrs. Rich went to her husband. "How is George?" was his first question. He expected her to say that he was dead. But she answered, "Come and see for yourself." And she led the way into the tent. On the approach of the two the lad looked up. General Rich was greatly astonished. What was the cause of this change? he wanted to know, and she replied, "Prayer and faith and trust in our heavenly Father." She told him what she had done. He was much affected by her story. From that hour George Patten began to mend, and before long he was about his work as usual. [16]

Patty Sessions — A Healer

*One of the great midwives of the early Church was Patty
Sessions. Her ministrations were both medical and spiritual.
The diary that she kept bears witness, like the diary of Eliza R.
Snow, to the spiritual gifts enjoyed by the sisters at Winter Quarters
and in their subsequent journeys. The following excerpts were
chosen for their references to healing and to other of the gifts as well.*

Wednesday, March 17, 1847. She [Mary Pierce] was buried. I went to
the funeral. Brigham Young preached. I visited sick. Mr. Sessions and
I went and laid hands to the widow Holman's daughter. She was healed.

Tuesday, March 30, 1847. Knit on another comforter. I was sent for to
go to Sister Leonard's. I went in the evening. They sent for Mr. Sessions.
We prayed, spoke in tongues, interpreted and prophesied and had a
good visit.

Thursday, April 1, 1847. Put Sarah, wife of Parley Pratt to bed. Visited
with Sister Knight at Sister Buel's. Mr. Sessions and I then visited the
sick. Anointed and laid hands on heads in blessings.

71

Tuesday, April 13, 1847. Visited Eliza R. Snow with Sister Leonard. Had
a good time, spoke in tongues, prophesied, and spirit of the Lord was
with us. I visited others that were sick also.

Saturday, May 1, 1847. Sylvia and I went to a meeting at Sister Leonard's.
Only females were there. We had a good meeting. I presided. It was
got by E. R. Snow. They spoke in tongues. I interpreted and some
prophesied.

Sunday, May 9, 1847. Went to Meeting. Council was given for the safety
of our cattle and also for raising a crop. In the evening I was sent
for and laid hands on Zina's child. We had a proper meeting.

Tuesday, May 18, 1847. Visited sick in several places, anointing and laying
hands on Sister Murray's son.

Thursday, June 3, 1847. Fair weather. We expected to start to move for
the mountains. I called to Sarah Ann's this evening with Eliza R. Snow.
Sisters Whitney and Kimball came in. We had a good time. Things
were given to us that we were not to tell of but to ponder them in
our hearts and profit thereby. And before we went down there E.
Beaman, E. Partridge and Zina Jacobs came and laid their hands upon
my head and blessed me, and so did Eliza R. Snow — thank the Lord. [17]

Zina And Eliza Minister Together

Amy Brown Lyman, eighth president of the Relief Society,
tells of an experience of healing that she observed as a child.

Among the outstanding events in our little town, which were especially interesting to women and girls, were the visits of Eliza R. Snow
and Zina D. H. Young, second and third general presidents of Relief
Society, respectively, both of whom I well remember. When they held
meetings in our community, all the women and girls who could possibly
attend did so, as did many of the children. Sister Snow had been president of all women's work in the Church and was well known and
beloved by M.I.A. girls and Primary children, as well as by mature
women.

My closest contact with Sisters Snow and Young was when they
came to our home on several occasions to bless and comfort my semi-
invalid mother. On one occasion we children were permitted in the
room and were allowed to kneel in prayer with these sisters, and later
to hear their fervent appeals for mother's recovery. They placed their
hands upon her head and promised that through our united faith she
would be spared to her family. This was an impressive spiritual experience for us, and the fulfillment of this promise was a testimony. [18]

72

"I Should Yet Administer To The Sick"

Mary B. Crandall tells of a prophecy that was fulfilled
by her assisting in the blessing of a sick sister.

I have seen prophecies fulfilled since I have been a member of the
Church. One I call to mind now. It happened this way: I was very
sick, almost unto death, when one night quite late I asked my son
to go and get some Elders to administer to me. He said he was afraid
every one would be in bed, but nevertheless he would go and try.
Soon he returned with three.

When they came into the bedroom I looked up and said to myself,
"One of you did not want to come." They surrounded the bed on
their knees. One of them anointed me, and the one that I thought
did not want to come asked the other to be mouth. After he got through,
he commenced, and such power and prophecies as he uttered! The
tears ran down his cheeks, and every one in the room was moved
to tears. One prophecy he made was I should get well and yet administer
to the sick. He said, "I did not want to come here tonight, but I have
got the blessing myself."

I had forgotten all about the circumstance till one day I was riding around town with Aunt Hannah Huntington and Aunt Zina. We stopped at a sister's who was sick. We had started for the buggy when some one asked Sister Zina to go back and bless the sick sister. I went, too. Sister Zina asked me to come and lay my hands on with her and Aunt Hannah, which I did, and so that prophecy was fulfilled, and many others I could relate, in such a simple way. [19]

Gift Of Healing To A Temple Worker

Bathsheba W. Smith, wife of George A. Smith (cousin
of the Prophet Joseph), was for years a devoted temple worker.
In her lifetime The Young Woman's Journal *wrote of her*
with great admiration.

Sister Smith worked about fourteen years in the Endowment House, which was erected in Salt Lake City for the accommodation of the Saints until a Temple could be built. President Young came over to her house one day and asked Sister Bathsheba if she would go and work in the Endowment House. She said yes, if her husband was willing. He had already given willing assent to the President, and thus her labors began. As long as work was done in the House Sister Smith was a faithful and constant worker in that House.

Sister Bathsheba speaks of many and marvelous healings wrought by the power of God and the faith of the Latter-day Saints in this holy House. So many, indeed, that memory will not retain one-tenth of the number.

One instance of a sister who came a cripple lifted out of a wagon, and who went out at the close of the day entirely healed. Another case, she says, she was reminded of when listening to some physicians talking the other day, who asserted that faith could not perform surgical operations. She wondered what it was that caused a circumstance of which she knew. A young girl from Payson came to the House with a knot of protruding veins or a swelling on one of her wrists. Sister Smith told her in blessing her that some day she should wake up and the swelling would all be gone. In prophesying this Sister Smith felt almost frightened at her own words. But it came to pass just as she said. If the cure was not a miracle, surely the prophecy was a very singular circumstance.

At another time a sister came who was blind in one eye, had been so since her childhood. She had been struck with a ruler by her teacher when a child, and the eye had been blind ever since. On coming into the House this sister gazed continually upon Sister Snow [Eliza R. evidently], and when asked at last what caused her deep attention, she told Sister Snow that she had seen her in a dream a little time before, and that she was to receive through her a great blessing. Sister Snow anointed the blind eye, and pronounced the healing of the Holy Spirit upon it. A few weeks afterwards the sister returned to show her once blind eye, which was now bright and perfectly sound. These are only a small number of the many and wonderful manifestations given in this place. [20]

Healing Gift Of Lucy B. Young

A wife of Brigham Young, Lucy B. Young was a "constant companion of Eliza R. Snow and Zina D. H. Young." When the St. George temple was dedicated in 1877, her name was the first on the roll of workers.

How many times the sick and suffering have come upon beds to that temple, and at once Sister Young would be called to take the afflicted one under her immediate charge, as all knew the mighty power she had gained through long years of fastings and prayers in the exercise of her special gift. When her hands are upon the head of another in blessing, the words of inspiration and personal prophecy that flow from her lips are like a stream of living fire. One sister who had not walked for twelve years was brought, and under the cheering faith of Sister Young she went through the day's ordinance and was perfectly healed of her affliction. Numbers of times childless women have sought out the prayers and faith of Sister Young in her temple duties, and have afterwards turned, as Hannah of old, to bring up their promised child to receive further blessings in the temple. Volumes would not contain the myriad instances of cases of illness and disease healed by the power of God under Sister Young's hands. No one was too high, none too low, no one too poor, no one too sick for her faith to reach. This gift is still with her, and humbly and powerfully does she exercise it. [21]

"I Have Never Seen A More Remarkable Faith Than Hers"

Apostle Melvin J. Ballard, whose mother received a revelation concerning him prior to his birth, tells of another instance of her exercising spiritual power on his behalf. This is a tribute he wrote to her for Mother's Day, shortly after her death.

Margaret McNeil Ballard, no son ever had a more faithful and devoted mother than mine, who not only demonstrated this after my coming to her, but before I was born, she desired me. Since I happened to be her youngest son in a family of eleven children, I being the seventh, she had enough children before I came to satisfy the ordinary mother. But that she did not forget me, but walked the lonely road to bring to me my glorious opportunity in earth life has made me love her almost to adoration.

Her faith and devotion is beautifully expressed in the last letter I ever received from her before her death, in 1918. This letter was dated December 31, 1917, in which she said,

> I do not know whether I ever told you of an experience I had when you were about thirteen years of age. You came out of your room and looked very strange. I spoke to you, but you did not answer me, and I took hold of you, and you had no power to speak. I laid you down on the lounge; your father was away. I was all alone, so I prayed over you. Then I anointed you with oil and prayed for you. I told the Lord that I had been of the impression before your birth that you would be a noble man and would fill a big mission on the earth, but if I was mistaken and if you were to go and leave the earth, it would be all right, I would do the best I could. But I felt that you had a work to do, so I said, "O God, if he is to live and be what I had been told, that I would dedicate you to the Lord, and I would never complain of what you had to do, nor would I do anything to hinder you, for you belong to Him and to no one else." So now, I repeat, "Let God use you in his work all the days of your life, for you belong to him, and I am proud that I was counted worthy to be your mother. I have tried to do the best I could under all circumstances.

She was a woman of unusual faith. I have never seen, among either men or women a more remarkable faith than hers. She had one outstanding purpose in all the activities of her life — to promote the welfare of the kingdom of God upon the earth. She was a positive character with unusual executive ability. I am grateful to have had such a heritage for my birthright from such a noble woman. [22]

To know
The welcome weight
Of hands on head,
Hear the sweet speech of promise,
And memorize the feeling
Of broken body
Blessed with healing —

Chapter Six

THE GIFT OF FAITH TO BE HEALED

" . . . He that hath faith in me to be healed, and is not appointed unto death, shall be healed."[1] Here are a few instances chosen from the lives of many, many early sisters who did indeed have "faith to be healed."

Arm Healed By The Prophet Joseph

Oliver B. Huntington relates one of the miracles that gave impetus to Joseph's name becoming known both for good and for ill.

Soon after Joseph settled in Kirtland and members of the Church began to gather to that place the name of Joseph Smith and his power with God aroused every body either for good or for bad and one Mrs. Johnson who lived at the town of Hyrum, 40 miles distant from Kirtland, heard of the wonderful man that could receive revelations from God, heal the sick and see angels — and he was called a prophet — she must see that prophet as she felt interested in such a man, such claims and such a power, both because she loved them and because she had a stiff arm that she wanted healed and made useful like the other, so she induced her husband John Johnson to take a journey to Kirtland to see the prophet and in an interview with him she asked the prophet to heal her arm.

Joseph asked her if she believed that God could make him instrumental in healing her arm which had been stiff a long time.

She answered that she believed her arm could be healed. The prophet only remarked that he would visit her the next day.

The next day Joseph came to Bishop N. K. Whitney's where Mr. Johnson and wife were staying and when he called in, there was a

Campbellite doctor and a Methodist preacher in the room — he took Mrs. Johnson by the hand without sitting down or standing on ceremonies, and after a very short mental prayer pronounced her arm whole in the name of Jesus Christ, and left the house immediately.

When he was gone the preacher asked if her arm was well. She immediately stretched out her arm straight, remarking at the same time "it's as well as the other."

The next day the preacher came to the house of Philo Dibble, who lived a little out of town and related what he saw and then tried to account for it upon natural principles saying that when Joseph pronounced the arm whole in the name of Jesus Christ it scared her so bad that it threw her in a heavy perspiration and relaxed the cords, and the result was that she could straighten her arm . . . .

When the knowledge of the miracle was had among the Saints some of the brethren asked the Prophet if the arm would remain sound. Joseph answered "the arm is as sound as the other and is as liable to accidents or to be hurt as the other."[2]

Lydia Knight And Joseph's Handkerchief

When the Saints were beginning to build Nauvoo, the challenge was enormous. The site for their "City Beautiful" was a malarial swamp.

Fevers of all kinds contracted in malarious countries were very prevalent. Great numbers of the strong — men and women who had borne every hardship without flinching, lay down in their beds and succumbed to the terrible disease. Ague dragged his shivering, shaking length from door to door, and there were not sufficient strong ones left to bury the dead. Specters instead of men crept slowly about laying those who were sleeping the last sleep in their dreary graves. Pestilence and fever were seated at every fireside. Even Joseph who had escaped from his enemies and came to Nauvoo, soon lay prostrate in his house, and even his yard was filled with the sick, the dying and the dead.

At last the spirit of the invincible Prophet rallied from this blow, and rising up by the power of God he commenced going about healing the sick. Hundreds were so healed; and as the brethren were healed they would arise and follow the Prophet continuing the glorious work. There was a change from this very day. The general health of the people began to improve.

Lydia had managed to wait upon her own ailing child and those of her neighbors who were the most helpless, notwithstanding her health was far from being good. Pale and weak she ministered unto those around her until September, when, worn out with her heavy labors and her body weakened by over-exertion, disease fastened itself upon her and she was prostrated.

For several days and nights she lay in a raging, burning fever, until it almost seemed as though her very flesh would be consumed upon her bones.

One day she called her husband to her bed and said:

"Newel, go and ask the Prophet to send me a handkerchief with his blessing."

"My dear wife, I do not like to trouble Joseph. You have no idea how worn down he is. He has asked the brethren to spare him as much as possible, for these constant never-ceasing calls upon him are depriving him of all his strength. I hope, my dear, you will soon be better."

The night came and passed and morning brought no relief to the weary sufferer.

Again she called Newel to her and entreated him to go to the Prophet and get a handkerchief with his blessing.

Newel went out, and in about half an hour returned, tied a handkerchief over her head saying:

"There, Lydia, is a handkerchief."

The sufferer experienced no relief from it, however, and rapidly grew worse.

A doctor was brought to her, and he tried his best to rally her, but all in vain. Thus one week passed.

One day Newel, seeing she was all but gone and was trying to speak to him, bent over her to catch the faint whisper,

"Newel, I am all but done with my suffering; good-by, dear one. You must do the best you can with the children. I cannot last much longer."

This was very brokenly whispered to the distracted man above her, who, as soon as she ceased, hurried away. Coming back soon, he called her; she knew him but was unable to reply.

"Here, Lydia, here is a handkerchief from the Prophet Joseph. Oh my wife, the one I brought before was not from him, I so hated to trouble him. But see this is from Joseph, and he says your Heavenly Father shall heal you, and you shall be restored to life and health."

The handkerchief was bound around her brow, and as it touched her head, the blessing sent with it, descended upon her; and over her and all through her was poured the spirit of healing. Sleep, so long a stranger to the poor afflicted one, closed her eye-lids in a quiet, restful, blessed slumber.

The hours came and fled, and in the quiet of midnight she awoke, and was like one who had been in a dark, loathsome dungeon, and was again free in the open air and sunshine. In the morning the physician came, and when he saw his patient, he exclaimed:

"Why, I never saw such a change in my life! That last medicine has worked like a charm, I wish I'd stayed and seen it operate. Her pulse is all right, her tongue is all right, and in fact she is comparatively a well woman."

After the doctor had praised up himself and his medicine to his heart's content, Newel quietly reached the bottle down from the shelf, and said:

"Sir, there is the medicine you speak of. My wife has not tasted one drop of it."

"But what's the meaning of all this change then?"

"She has been healed by faith through the Prophet Joseph Smith."

After studying some time over the matter the doctor said:

"Well it's a good thing to get well on any terms." [3]

"She Arose In Faith"

B. F. Johnson relates the story of the miraculous healing of
his sister Nancy, not performed for those who sought a sign, but
in the due time of the Lord.

About the year 1830, when I was twelve years of age, Nancy, my eldest sister, was thrown from a horse, and had her hip broken.

The bone was broken so near the socket that it could not be set, and physicians all agreed that it would be impossible for her ever again to walk upon that leg, or in any degree to recover its use, as ossification had taken place without a connection of the bones and they had slipped past each other, making the broken limb nearly an inch shorter than the other. She walked upon two crutches, and for years was not able to bring upon the broken limb weight sufficient to hurt the finger of a small child, if placed under her foot.

In the year 1831, my brothers Joel H. and David received the gospel in Amherst, Ohio, and in the fall of the same year my brother David brought to us the Book of Mormon, near Fredonia, State of New York.

Soon afterwards my brother Joel, with A. W. Babbitt — then only a boy, came also, and was followed by Elders Brackinbury and Durfee. Elder Brackinbury was an earnest and powerful preacher, and all the Elders seemed filled with the spirit of the Lord. Many received their testimony, and my mother and Lyman R. Shearman, a brother-in-law, were the first to be baptized.

Priest and people came out to oppose the work, and would scoffingly ask, "Why, if miracles can be performed, do you not heal Sister Nancy?" Many would also say: "If they would only heal Sister Nancy we would all believe!"

My sister was a young woman of excellent mind and character. Having a good common education, she had for some years taught our district summer school, and, being religiously inclined, had joined the Freewill Baptist church. Like my mother, who was also a religious woman, she was not only respected, but was beloved by all who knew her. But, although she had obeyed the gospel, the time had not come for her release from her crutches by the healing power of God. The wicked were seeking it for a sign, as in the days of our Savior, when they followed Him even to His crucifixion, demanding that He come down from the cross, as a sign, to prove to them that He was the Son of God; yet no sign was given except that of their overthrow and destruction. . . .

[Two years later when we had moved to Kirtland] the Spirit of the Lord seemed to be poured out upon the Saints. There families often met together to "speak of the Lord," and the gifts of the gospel were enjoyed in rich abundance. As yet my sister Nancy had never, since her hip had been broken, taken one step unaided by her crutches; but the time had now come for her release.

81

She was commanded by Elder Jared Carter — then a man of mighty faith — to arise, leave her crutches and walk.

She arose in faith, full of joy, and was from that hour made whole, and never again did she walk upon crutches or lean upon a staff.[4]

Healed By A Missionary Through Faith In Christ

An incident in the life of David W. Patten is related by a missionary companion.

I think Elder David W. Patten possessed the gift of healing to a greater degree than any man I ever associated with. I remember on one occasion when I was laboring with him as a missionary in Tennessee, he was sent for to administer to a woman who had been sick for five years and bed-ridden for one year and not able to help herself. Brother Patten stepped to her bedside and asked her if she believed in the Lord, Jesus Christ. She replied that she did. He then took her by the hand and said, "In the name of Jesus Christ, arise!"

She immediately sat up in bed, when he placed his hands upon her head and rebuked her disease, pronounced blessings upon her head and promised that she should bear children. She had been married for several years and had never had any children, and this promise seemed very unlikely ever to be fulfilled. But she arose from her bed immediately, walked half a mile to be baptized and back again in her wet clothes. She was healed from that time, and within one year became a mother, and afterwards bore several children. [5]

Gifts Enjoyed In The British Mission

The various gifts of the Spirit appear to have been enjoyed in England as much as anywhere in the Church. Bishop George Halliday, who labored extensively as a missionary in his native country, participated in a remarkable healing.

Upon a warm Sunday evening, after he had been preaching to an audience in Bristol, he was accosted by a Mrs. Ware, a sister in the Church, who told him she had a son extremely sick and thought to be dying. She begged him to go home with her and administer to it. She lived three miles distant, on Durham Down. It was quite late in the evening and he was so extremely tired that he scarcely felt able to comply with her request; and yet he did not like to decline. All at once he felt impressed to say: "Here, Sister Ware, you take my handkerchief and go home to your child and lay it on him wherever he seems to be affected, praying to the Lord to heal him. If you do this I will promise you that he will recover."

With full faith the good lady took the handkerchief and departed. On reaching her home she was met at the door by her daughters and friends, who informed her that her son was dead.

"No," said she, "I cannot believe it! Brother Halliday has promised me that he shall live, and I have his handkerchief to lay upon him."

She hastened to the boy and did as she had been directed to, and the child, which a few minutes before had been inanimate, began to show signs of life. The next morning he was able to come down to breakfast, and soon regained his wonted health. He afterwards emigrated to Utah. [6]

Wife Of Wilford Woodruff Restored To Life

A number of instances have been related upon good authority of persons actually returning from the spirit world when faith to heal and to be healed has been sufficiently strong. Such a case is recorded by Wilford Woodruff.

December 3rd found my wife very low. I spent the day taking care of her, and the following day I returned to Eaton to get some things for her. She seemed to be gradually sinking, and in the evening her spirit apparently left her body and she was dead. The sisters gathered around her body, weeping, while I stood looking at her in sorrow. The spirit and power of God began to rest upon me, until for the first time during her illness, faith filled my soul, although she lay before me as one dead. I had some oil. I took it and consecrated it before the Lord for anointing the sick. I then bowed before the Lord and prayed for the life of my companion, and I anointed her with oil in the name of the Lord, and I laid my hands upon her, and in the name of Jesus Christ I rebuked the power of death and the destroyer and commanded the same to depart from her, and the spirit of life to enter her body. Her spirit returned to her body from that hour, and she was made whole.

We all felt to praise the name of God and to trust in Him and keep His commandments. While this experience was going on with me, my wife related afterwards that her spirit left her body and she saw her body lying upon the bed, and the sisters weeping. She looked at them and at me and upon the babe, and while gazing upon this scene, two personages came into the room carrying a coffin and told her they had come for her body. One of these messengers informed her that she could have the privilege of returning to her tabernacle and continuing in her body. The condition was if she felt she could stand by her husband and with him pass through all the cares, trials, tribulations, and afflictions of life which he would be called to pass through for the gospel's sake unto the end. When she looked at the situation of her husband and child, she said, "Yes, I will do it." At the moment that decision was made, the power of faith rested upon me, and when I administered to her, her spirit entered her tabernacle and she saw the messengers carry the coffin out through the door. [7]

83

Healings In Hawaii

In relating his missionary experiences in Hawaii, George Q. Cannon tells of some interesting experiences of the sisters exercising faith to be healed.

The Lord blessed the natives who joined the Church in many ways, and they rejoiced exceedingly in the gifts of the Spirit. One day . . . Brother Napela and some of the other native Saints had visited a woman who believed in the gospel, who wished to be baptized; she had been unable to walk upright for five years, but she was anxious for them to administer to her, that she might be restored. They laid their hands upon her and commanded her in the name of the Lord Jesus Christ, to arise and walk. She immediately stood up and walked, and went and was baptized.

This created quite an excitement in the neighborhood, for she was well known, and the people were much astonished at her restoration. The attention of numbers were turned to the gospel by this occurrence.

Another instance which happened about the same time was that of a woman who was a member of the Presbyterian church. She was afflicted with dropsy, or something very like that disease. She had tried various remedies, but obtained no relief. She had heard about the gifts in the Church, and she called upon Brothers Napela and Uaua to administer to her, saying she was willing to covenant and foresake her sins. They administered to her and she was healed; all the swelling left her and she was baptized. On Sunday she attended meeting, and afterwards made some remarks derogatory to the work, indulging in a spirit of apostasy; her disease returned immediately, and she was as bad as ever.

Another instance was that of a woman, one of whose limbs was withered, and who was afflicted with palsy. She was baptized, and was speedily restored to health.

A niece of hers was afterwards afflicted similarly; she requested us to administer to her, and when we did so, she was restored to health. [8]

Zina's Faith In Her Own Behalf

Many stories are told of Zina D. H. Young blessing the lives of other people. Here is a case in which she sought and received a blessing for herself, and subsequently inspired another sister. It is related by Oliver B. Huntington.

I remember hearing our precious Aunt Zina tell how she had been afflicted with the toothache for many years, it remaining sometimes for months with no cessation. Finally, she was once worn out with it, and sent for the elders to come and rebuke it, saying she never wanted it to return. The administration was performed, and from that day to this she has never had the toothache again. And, too, she yet has most of her teeth remaining. At the time of her healing she was twenty-nine years old.

Another lady heard her tell the same story. She thought she wished she only had such faith. Ever since she was a girl of ten years she had suffered off and on with the worst form of toothache. She did indeed try to exercise faith to be healed at various times, but with only temporary success. One day she was utterly discouraged and worn out, for she had done every thing, even to having a tooth extracted, to be relieved of the terrible pain, but all in vain. She sat in her room, in great pain and misery. Suddenly she remembered she, too, was just twenty-nine years old, and she resolved to send for some of the best elders she could get, and see if her faith would be as great as was Aunt Zina's. Her husband called in two elders, and together they administered to the afflicted one. She was healed at once, and what is far better she received the same permanent gift that had been bestowed upon Sister Zina, and was never again so tormented. [9]

"There Has Been A Council Held In Heaven"

*Susa Young Gates was one of the most accomplished of the early
Mormon women. She wrote nine books, was very much involved
in politics and education, and was an active worker for
woman's rights. After the incident described below, she also went
to the Salt Lake Temple daily and wrote the first Mormon
genealogical treatises. On her deathbed, speaking with
great effort, she recounted the story of her being preserved
to do that work.*

In the midst of rearing a family of thirteen children, writing, editing
magazines, I was sent as sole delegate from the National Council of
the United States to the meeting of the International Council of Women
held in Copenhagen. On my return journey I was taken seriously sick
at Lake Geneva, and was confined for weeks in the home of a distinguished friend. I finally succeeded in getting a message to the Elders,
and Levi Edgar Young came and blessed me. I recovered sufficiently
to get to London. Here President Francis M. Lyman and Elder Henry
H. Blood administered to me. President Lyman, as spokesman, was
in the act of dedicating me to the Lord, and telling me I should not
fear to die, for there was a great work for me in the spirit world, and
I could do as much good there as here. Suddenly he stopped, and
after pausing for about two minutes continued with these words, "There
has been a council held in heaven, and it has been decided you shall
live to perform temple work, and you shall do a greater work than
you have ever done before."

I managed to get home after that, but for two years or more I was
an invalid, so emaciated that I looked more like a skeleton than a human
being. A prominent Doctor told my husband that I had not one chance
in a hundred to live. One day my mother asked if I would like to
have Patriarch William White administer to me. I said, "I don't want
him to come and dedicate me to the Lord, for I want to live." He came
and stood at the foot of my bed. I cried out to him, "I don't want
to die, I want to live — to live to do temple work!" He said, "Well,
Sister, if you want to live to do temple work, you shall live."

They brought me, as I began to gain strength, to the temple in a
chair. I weighed only 85 lbs., and was terribly weak. Brothers John
Nicholson and Joseph Christenson blessed me and promised, "Aunt
Susie, you shall live until you are wholly satisfied with life."[10]

Healed Of Tuberculosis Of The Spine

*Many conditions that have been medically hopeless have been
completely cured by faith. An event that happened in 1897
is related by Sister Ahena R. Hodson.*

Many years ago, when I was a girl eighteen years of age, I had
tuberculosis of the spine. For three years I had not been able to walk
and had to be pushed around in a wheel chair. I was living at home
with the family at Provo, Utah, at the time. Mother brought me to
the Salt Lake Temple to be administered to. I was so helpless that I
had to be carried about and my weight was reduced to but sixty-five
pounds. I had been administered to twice with little or no change in
my condition. President Heber J. Grant, then an apostle, sealed the
anointing in the third administration. In his blessing, among other things,
he said, "You shall grow up to be a living monument of God's goodness
and mercy unto His people in this day and generation, and you shall
become a mother in Israel."

Two other administrations followed this one. In the last, Brother
Adolph Madsen, Brother Elijah F. Sheets and others, whose names
I do not remember, assisted in the ordinance. When the administration
was over, mother came to carry me out of the room and put me into
my chair in the hall, where I was to stay until one of the brethren
could carry me out of the Temple. As she was taking me in her arms,
I pushed her away and walked out of the room into the hall by my
own strength. I shall never forget the sensation that came over me.
I felt as if I had been touched with an electric current. My blood ran
through my veins like fire and a feeling of great strength possessed
my body. A breathless silence filled the room when I stood up and
walked. Astonishment possessed the heart of every one present. As
I stepped forth, I seemed to be lifted up. As I passed through the door
I looked back into the room and among all those present, I saw but
one person, Brother Madsen. He stood as if petrified and appeared
as white as snow. And then, out of the stillness of that Holy moment,
came the joyful voice of mother, "Praise God! She can walk!"

My bones were very soft and, at the advice of the brethren, I got
some crutches. I used these for two years, my legs getting stronger
all the while. From then on, I walked and danced and ran with a joy
that is beyond the power of words to tell. No one can ever know the
ecstasy and gratitude that filled my soul when the use of my limbs
was restored to me, unless, he too, had suffered a like loss of health
and had it returned again.

I married later and am now the mother of three children, all of
whom are grown. My name was Ahena C. Reese, daughter of George
K. Reese. This event happened in the year 1897. It was the talk of
Provo, and many people came to see the change that had taken place
in my condition. A record of this circumstance was made in the temple. [11]

Dying Maori Woman Healed

A missionary to New Zealand, Amasa Aldrich, recalls an interesting healing in which he took part.

It used to be the custom of the Maori people, and may be so today, to remove a person who is believed to be in a dying condition, into a tent some distance from the village. In this isolated shelter he remains until death comes to his release.

As a missionary, I arrived at a Maori village on the 24th day of April, 1885. There were no members of the Church residing there, although there were those among them who knew of the teachings of the Latter-day Saints and were more or less friendly.

One of the old women of the village was very sick and had been taken to the tent some distance from the settlement.

The Chief of the village learned of my being there and came to see me. He asked me if I would administer to a person who did not belong to our church. I told him I would be glad to do so if the person had faith in Christ and also believed in the healing principle of administration.

He took me to the tent and many of the people of the village followed us. When we entered the tent, the Chief explained who I was and told the natives that I was willing to administer to a person not of our Church, on condition that he had faith. The old woman was glad I came and, when I asked her if she believed in Christ and if she wished me to administer to her, she said she did believe and that she was full of faith and desired me to offer a prayer that she might be healed.

I administered to her as she requested, after which we all returned to the village. The next morning when I arose, the tent was gone. I asked the Chief why the tent had been taken away and with much joy he told me that the woman was well and had gone back to her home. [12]

87

To wake
In Satan's long midnight
And command it to be done,
Dispelling dark
By invocation of the sun —

Chapter Seven

THE GIFT OF POWER OVER EVIL SPIRITS

In addressing the Relief Society in Nauvoo, Joseph Smith showed the sisters how they would come in possession of "the privileges, blessings and gifts of the priesthood, and that the signs should follow them, such as healing the sick, casting out devils, etc." He did not indicate that a special ordination would bring them these gifts, but that they would attain them "by a virtuous life, and conversation, and diligence in keeping all the commandments." [1]

Incidents of casting out devils appear to be less common than incidents involving the exercise of other spiritual gifts, judging by what has been recorded. The following three stories, however, show that some of the sisters did, when the need arose, call upon the powers of heaven to triumph over evil spirits.

"The Power Of The Devil Was Destroying Our Peace"

*Sarah S. Leavitt's journal shows her as a woman who was
never slow to respond to the needs of the moment. She acted
in full faith and obtained the results she desired.*

We swapped farms with a man, got one by the big mound, seven miles from [Nauvoo], a fine pleasant place. But Priscilla was born before we moved and we had much sickness. There was four of the boys all sick at once with the black canker. There were many who died in Nauvoo with the same disorder and some of my boys were brought to the very gate of death, to all appearances. But by watching over them day and night and administering, the Lord raised them up, thanks be to his Holy name.

One of the boys had got about and could walk out while the other lay at the point of death. We had to watch over him every moment. The one that could walk as soon as he lay down at night he took with the toothache and would roll and groan. After a few nights (I had laid down to rest a few moments) he began to groan. I had a strange feeling come over me. I thought it was the power of the devil that was destroying our peace, and I had bore it as long as I would. I jumped out of the bed with about the same feeling I would have to drive a hog out of the house, and as sure he would have to go. I stepped up very spry to the bed and put my hands on his head in the name of Jesus and asked God to rebuke the spirit. I did not say a loud word, but as soon as it was done he went to sleep and never was troubled any more.

I had administered to very many to rebuke disease, but never had the same feeling before or since. [2]

"Satan Desired To Clip My Glory"

Helen Mar Kimball Whitney lost a baby at Winter Quarters and was herself near to death. Through the faith of her father and mother, Heber C. and Vilate Kimball, she was preserved.

For three months I lay, a portion of the time like one dead they told me; but that did not last long. I was alive to my spiritual condition and dead to the world . . . .

During that season I lost my speech, forgot the names of everybody and everything, and was living in another sphere, learning lessons that would serve me in future times to keep me in the narrow way. I was left a poor wreck of what I had been, but the Devil, with all his cunning, little thought that he was fitting and preparing my heart to fulfill its destiny. My father said that Satan desired to clip my glory, and was quite willing I should die happy; but when he was thwarted he tried in every possible way to destroy my tabernacle.

President Young said that the mountains through which we passed were filled with the spirits of the Gadianton robbers spoken of in the *Book of Mormon*. The Lord gave father faith enough to hold me until I was capable of exercising it for myself. I was so weak that I was often discouraged in trying to pray, as the evil spirits caused me to feel that it was no use; but the night after the first Christmas in this valley, I had my last struggle and resolved that they should buffet me no longer.

I fasted for one week, and every day I gained till I had won the victory and I was just as sensible of the presence of holy spirits around my bedside as I had been of the evil ones. It would take up too much room to relate my experience with the spirits, but New Year's eve, after spending one of the happiest days of my life, I was moved upon to talk to my mother. I knew her heart was weighed down in sorrow and I was full of the Holy Ghost. I talked as I never did before; I was too weak to talk with such a voice (of my own strength), besides I never before spoke with such eloquence, and she knew that it was not myself. She was so affected that she sobbed till I ceased. [3]

Sister Grant Silences The Planchette

Heber J. Grant tells of an unusual experience in which he watched his mother exercise spiritual powers.

When I was a little boy my mother gained her livelihood by going out sewing. She used to sew, not five hours a day, which some people now consider a day's work, but she would sew all day and sometimes till late at night. When she continued her sewing into the evening it was always understood, that I being her only child, should come and take supper with her, and then we would go home together.

In the home of the late William S. Godbe, on the corner of Second East and Second South street, in a building known as the "Octagon House" — which still stands there with its eight sides — my mother was sewing in one room while a number of people were having a hilarious time in the parlor, receiving messages from a planchette. They had their hands on this little machine and it was running around writing messages. These people were laughing and joking and having a fine time.

They wanted mother to come in there but she would not go. Her statement was that President Brigham Young had said: "Let that thing alone. It will deliver a message to some of you that will lead you on to apostasy. Those who are fooling with it will apostatize if they do not repent." And scores of them did apostatize. They joined what was known as the Godbeite movement, largely as a result of the messages they had received by this planchette.

Finally they jokingly said that if mother would not come in where they were, they would bring the machine in where she was sewing. They brought their machine but it did not work. Then they took it into the other room and it worked as before. Then they begged mother to go in there. To my surprise she went; but while she was there they could not make it work.

When we got home I said to her: "Mother, why did you go into the parlor when Brother Brigham had told the people not to go near that machine?" She said: "My boy, I went in there to keep it from working, and not out of curiosity. When they brought it into the room where I was, I prayed to the Lord that as I was not going where it was he would not permit it to work in my presence. When they invited me to go into the parlor I told the Lord if he would give me the impression that it would not work in my presence I would go in there and shut it up. I did not go out of curiosity; and as you know, it did not work while I was there."[4]

92

All these
And the other good gifts —

In our hands lies one or more,
A legitimate inheritance.

And when they have
Given us living bread,
Let us not return it unused,
A stone instead.

Gratitude is extended to the Church Historical Department for permission to use the documents that are listed below as found in the Church Archives. Special thanks is given to Church Historian Leonard Arrington for his personal help and suggestions toward the writing of this book.

The author wishes to indicate that when dealing with manuscript sources she has taken the liberty of supplying correct spelling and punctuation.

NOTES

Chapter One

1. Moroni 10:24.
2. James E. Talmage, *The Articles of Faith* (Salt Lake City: Deseret News, 1899), p. 236.
3. D&C 4:10.
4. *Lectures On Faith* (Salt Lake City: N. B. Lundwall, n.d.), p. 8.
5. Nauvoo Relief Society Minutes, 17 March 1842 to 18 March 1844, pp. 23, 24, Church Archives, Historical Department, The Church of Jesus Christ of Latter-day Saints (hereafter referred to as Church Archives).
6. *Woman's Exponent*, 41 (March 1913), 46.
7. As quoted by Harold B. Lee, *Conference Reports*, October 1955, p. 56.
8. Susa Young Gates Papers, Miscellaneous History File, p. 21, Church Archives.
9. Matthew Cowley, *Matthew Cowley Speaks* (Salt Lake City: Deseret Book Company, 1954), p. 414.

Chapter Two

1. B. H. Roberts, ed., *History of the Church of Jesus Christ of Latter-day Saints*, 7 vols., 2nd ed. rev. (Salt Lake City: Deseret Book Company, 1957), I, 323.
2. Nauvoo Relief Society Minutes, 17 March 1842 to 18 March 1844, pp. 19, 20, Church Archives.
3. Roberts, ed., *History of the Church*, V, 31, 32.
4. Zina D. H. Young, "How I Gained My Testimony Of The Truth," *Young Woman's Journal*, 4 (April 1893), 318, 319.
5. "A Distinguished Woman: Zina D. H. Young," *Woman's Exponent*, 10 (15 December 1881), 107.
6. *Lydia Knight's History* (Salt Lake City: Juvenile Instructor Office, 1883), pp. 21, 22.
7. Jane Elizabeth Manning James, Autobiography, MS, Church Archives.
8. Matthias F. Cowley, *Wilford Woodruff* (Salt Lake City: Deseret News, 1909), p. 355.
9. Andrew Jenson, *Latter-day Saint Biographical Encyclopedia*, 4 vols. (Salt Lake City: Andrew Jenson History Company, 1901), III, 563, 564.
10. Salt Lake Stake Relief Society Record 1880 to 1892, p. 13, Church Archives.
11. *Biography of Ann Howell Burt* (Brigham City, Utah: Privately published, 1916), pp. 14, 15.
12. From the memoire of Henry Savage and Family, by Nephi Miles Savage, pp. 17, 18, as quoted in Ogden Kraut, *The Gift of Tongues* (Published by the author, n.d.), pp. 43, 44.
13. *Eliza R. Snow: An Immortal* (Salt Lake City: Nicholas G. Morgan, Sr., Foundation, 1957), pp. 322, 323.
14. Ibid., p. 360.
15. Edward W. Tullidge, *The Women of Mormondom* (New York: 1877), pp. 475-477.
16. Irene King Read, *Sense and Nonsense, My Life Story* (Privately published, n.d.), pp. 22, 23.
17. "A Sketch of Pioneer Life in Utah," *Juvenile Instructor*, 19 (1 February 1884), 35, 36.
18. John A. Widtsoe, *In The Gospel Net* (Salt Lake City: Improvement Era Book, 1941), p. 89.
19. *The Story of Edwin Marion Whiting and Anna Maria Isaacson* Provo, Utah: J. Grant Stevenson, 1969), p. 153.
20. Interview with Douglas Todd, Jr., November 1969, as found in Kraut, pp. 77-79.

Chapter Three

1. Acts 21:9.
2. Talmage, p. 232.
3. Matthias Cowley, *Wilford Woodruff*, p. 228.
4. "Women Past and Present," *Woman's Exponent*, 41 (Midwinter 1913), 37.
5. Lucy Mack Smith, *History of Joseph Smith* (Salt Lake City: Bookcraft, 1958), p. 291.
6. Ibid., pp. 203-205.
7. Roberts, ed., I, p. 101.
8. John Henry Evans, *Charles Coulson Rich* (New York: The Macmillan Company, 1936, pp. 38-40.
9. *Scraps of Biography* (Salt Lake City: Juvenile Instructor Office, 1883), pp. 41, 42.
10. Tullidge, pp. 344-349.
11. Salt Lake Stake Relief Society Record 1880 to 1882, p. 35, Church Archives.
12. "Carrie M. C. Smith," *Young Woman's Journal*, 7 (March 1896), 277.
13. Heber J. Grant, *Conference Reports*, 3 April 1927, pp. 17, 18.
14. Jeremiah Stokes, *Modern Miracles* (Salt Lake City: Deseret Book Company, 1935), pp. 175-179.
15. Mary Jacobs Wilson to the author, 4 February 1973.
16. Matthew Cowley, p. 244.

Chapter Four

1. "Nauvoo Conference Minutes," *Millennial Star*, 5 (January 1845), 117.
2. Tullidge, pp. 107-109.
3. Jenson, I, p. 267.
4. "Our Picture Gallery," *Young Woman's Journal*, 2 (March 1891), 292, 293.
5. Tullidge, pp. 207-209.
6. *Sarah S. Leavitt Journal*, copied from her history by Juanita Leavitt Pulsipher (n.p., 1919), p. 16.
7. *Eliza R. Snow: An Immortal*, p. 6.
8. Zina Young, pp. 317, 318.
9. "Past Three Score Years and Ten," *Young Woman's Journal*, 12 (October 1901), 440.
10. Preston Nibley, *L.D.S. Stories of Faith and Courage* (Salt Lake City: Bookcraft, 1957), pp. 141, 142.
11. Hannah Cornaby, *Autobiography And Poems* (Salt Lake City: J. C. Graham & Company, 1881), pp. 13, 14.
12. Tullidge, pp. 122-128.
13. Wilford Woodruff Journal, 2 July 1840, Wilford Woodruff Collection, Church Archives.
14. Augusta Joyce Crocheron, *Representative Women of Deseret* (Salt Lake City: J. C. Graham & Company, 1884), pp. 99-101.
15. Jenson, I, p. 695.
16. Preston Nibley, *Faith Promoting Stories* (Salt Lake City: Deseret Book Company, 1943), pp. 137, 138.
17. *Lydia Knight's History*, pp. 71, 72.
18. "F[emale] R[elief] Society Reports," *Woman's Exponent*, 1 (July 1872), 18.
19. *Deacons Course of Study* (Salt Lake City: Church of Jesus Christ of Latter-day Saints, 1917), pp. 24-26.
20. "Prophetic Sayings of Heber C. Kimball to Sister Amanda H. Wilcox" (n.p., n.d.), pp. 1-3.
21. Aurelia Spencer Rogers, *Life Sketches* (Salt Lake City: Geo. Q. Cannon & Sons Company, 1898), pp. 169, 170.
22. Bryant S. Hinckley, *Sermons and Missionary Services of Melvin Joseph Ballard* (Salt Lake City: Deseret Book Company, 1949), pp. 22, 23.

23. Ibid., p. 18.

24. Floy L. Turner, *Lorena Eugenia Washburn Larsen: A Mother In Israel* (Provo, Utah: J. Grant Stevenson, 1969), p. 70.

25. Ibid., pp. 65-67.

26. Susa Young Gates, "More Than A Halo," *Juvenile Instructor*, 42 (15 November 1907), 683, 684.

27. Bryant S. Hinckley, *Heber J. Grant, Highlights in the Life of a Great Leader* (Salt Lake City: Deseret Book Company, 1951), p. 243.

28. *Scraps of Biography*, pp. 73-75.

Chapter Five

1. James 5:14.

2. Blessing given to Eda Rogers by Joseph Smith, Sr., copied by the Noah Rogers Family Association, a copy in possession of the author.

3. Roberts, ed., IV, p. 607.

4. Gates, History Note headed "28 February — Headquarters Meeting," Susa Young Gates Papers, Church Archives.

5. "A Leaf From An Autobiography," *Woman's Exponent*, 7 (15 November 1878), 91.

6. *Journal of Discourses* (Liverpool, 1854-1886, rpt. 1967), XIII, 155.

7. Roberts, ed., VI, p. 322.

8. Salt Lake Stake Relief Society Record 1880 to 1882, p. 160, Church Archives.

9. Ibid., p. 233.

10. "Questions and Answers," *Improvement Era*, 10 (February 1907), 308. (Quoted also in *Selections from Answers to Gospel Questions*, A Course of Study for the Melchizedek Priesthood Quorums, 1972-73, p. 200.)

11. Francis W. Kirkham, *A New Witness for Christ in America* (Salt Lake City: Utah Printing Company, 1960), I, 104.

12. Nauvoo Relief Society Minutes, 17 March 1842 to 18 March 1844, p. 19, Church Archives.

13. *Sarah S. Leavitt Journal*, pp. 9, 10.

14. Tullidge, p. 169.

15. Kate B. Carter, *Heart Throbs of the West* (Salt Lake City: Daughters of Utah Pioneers, 1947), VIII, 233.

16. Evans, pp. 119-121.

17. Patty Sessions Diary, typescript, pp. 27-33, Church Archives.

18. Amy Brown Lyman, *In Retrospect* (Salt Lake City: Deseret News Press, 1945), p. 38.

19. "Autobiography of a Noble Woman," *Young Woman's Journal*, 6 (September 1895), 552, 553.

20. "Sketch of Sister Bathsheba W. Smith," *Young Woman's Journal*, 4 (April 1893), 295, 296.

21. "Sketch of the Labors of Sister Lucy B. Young in the Temples," *Young Woman's Journal*, 4 (April 1893), 299.

22. Hinckley, *Sermons and Missionary Services of Melvin Joseph Ballard*, pp. 26, 27.

Chapter Six

1. D&C 42:48.

2. "Our Sunday Chapter," *Young Woman's Journal*, 2 (February 1891), 225, 226.

3. *Lydia Knight's History*, pp. 52-55.

4. *Early Scenes in Church History* (Salt Lake City: Juvenile Instructor Office, 1882), pp. 9-11.

5. Ibid., p. 29.

6. Ibid., p. 32.

7. Wilford Woodruff, *Leaves From My Journal* (Salt Lake City: The Deseret News, 1909), p. 52.

8. George Q. Cannon, *My First Mission* (Salt Lake City: Juvenile Instructor Office, 1879), pp. 63, 64.

9. "Our Sunday Chapter," *Young Woman's Journal*, 2 (November 1890), 78.

10. "Susa Young Gates," *Utah Genealogical and Historical Magazine*, 24 (July 1933), 98, 99.

11. Stokes, pp. 57-60.

12. Ibid., pp. 44-46.

Chapter Seven

1. Roberts, ed., IV, 602.

2. *Sarah S. Leavitt Journal*, p. 21.

3. Crocheron, pp. 112, 113.

4. *Deseret News*, 24 April 1920, Section 4, p. 8.